ON ROMANTICISM IN SLAVIC LITERATURE

MUSAGETES

CONTRIBUTIONS TO THE HISTORY OF
SLAVIC LITERATURE AND CULTURE

Edited by

DMITRIJ ČIŽEVSKIJ

Heidelberg

I

MOUTON & CO · 'S-GRAVENHAGE

1957

ON ROMANTICISM
IN
SLAVIC LITERATURE

by

DMITRIJ ČIŽEVSKIJ

Heidelberg

Chyzevs'kyĭ, Dmytro

MOUTON & CO · 'S-GRAVENHAGE

1957

Printed in The Netherlands by Mouton & Co, Printers, The Hague

CONTENTS

I

INTRODUCTION

Much has been written about European romanticism, but dis-
proportionately less about Slavic romanticism,[1] although its significance for the development of Slavic national consciousness is
so manifest that it is nearly always discussed without proof, without
the adduction of factual material, and with no small number of
mistakes! Thus, Goethe and Schiller are almost always named
among the romanticists, and Hegel among the philosophers of
romanticism, together with Fichte and Schelling, although he was
in fact the author of sharply unfavorable criticism of romanticism.
Assertions are continually repeated to the effect that all Slavo-
philes, including Konstantin Aksakov and Jurij Samarin, were influenced by the philosophy of Schelling, whereas both these Slavo-
philes were Hegelians. The Ukrainian classicists are considered

[1] In particular there are very few synthetic Slavic works. The majority os
works on Slavic romanticism is devoted to individual writers or problemf.
A survey of old literature is given in the book of I. Máchal, *Slovanské literatury*,
II (Prague, 1925). The book of M. Zdziechowski, *Byron i jego wiek*, 2 vols.
(1895–7), narrows the concept of romanticism, as do other works on Slavic
"Byronism". M. Szyjkowski, *Polski romantyzm w czeskim życiu duchownym*
(Poznań, 1947), speaks only of Polish and Czech romanticism, but very little
space is devoted in this book to theoretic analysis. – I. Zamotin wrote of
Russian romanticism in *Romantizm 20-x godov XIX veka v russkoj literature*
(SPb., 1909; 2nd edition SPb., 1911–13); in spite of the weakness of this book's
analyses, one must condiser the symposium edited by A. Beleckij, *Russkij
romantizm* (1927), and the book of B. Mejlach, *Puškin i russkij romantizm*
(Moscow, 1937), to be even weaker. A great deal of valuable raw material is
given in P. Sakulin, *Iz istorii russkogo idealizma. Knjaz' V. F. Odoevskij*, 2 vols.
(M., 1913). The most interesting material is to be found in works on the
Polish romanticists, for example in J. Kleiner, *Mickiewicz*, 2 vols. (Lublin,
1948).

romanticists, and the Czech romanticist Erben a classicist.... All the inaccuracies and errors cannot be recounted here.[2] The influence of Soviet scholarship has proved to be particularly harmful to historico-literary research. Soviet literary historians, proceeding from a completely unclear concept of "realism" and from the dogmatic recognition of "socialist realism" as the only "progressive" style, try to proclaim all the great writers of the past "realists", although there may not be the slightest basis for such an assertion. Having mastered the history of Russian and Ukrainian literature, Soviet scholarship is now beginning to penetrate into the literary history of other Slavic peoples: even the works of the Polish romanticists (the most consistent representatives of romanticism among the Slavs) are now starting to be interpreted either as works of "classicism" or as "early realism"...[3]

I shall not concern myself here with the characteristics of romanticism as an entire movement, to which subject I devoted several pages in my *Outline of Comparative Slavic Literatures*.[4] I shall instead follow another route, that of investigating separate motifs of Slavic romantic literatures. But first a preliminary remark is necessary.

Two characteristics of literary motifs are known to every literary historian who has had occasion to deal with diverse literatures. In the first place, literary motifs reappear in various epochs, among various peoples, among writers of various artistic individualities. Secondly, these recurrent motifs are notable for their stability: many of them appear in the same forms, with the same details, in the most various literary works.[5] Both of these characteristics of

[2]   Zamotin's book, cited in footnote 1, gives in the first volume a characterization of the ideology of romanticism in which are united mutually contradictory features. A great many works are limited to indications of Byron's influence, whereas his poetry, of course, is only one of the episodes, and a late one at that, in the history of European romanticism.

[3]   *Cf.* for example W. Kubacki, *Pierwiosnki polskiego romantyzmu* (Kraków, 1949), and M. Jastruń, *Mickiewicz* (1949; 5th edition 1952). Cf. W. Weintraub's review in *Wiadomości*, No. 487, July 5, 1955.

[4]   My book, *Outline of Comparative Slavic Literatures* (Boston, 1953), pp. 85–93.

[5]   The repetition of motifs in different writers played a significant role in the once fashionable search for "influences" and "borrowings". However, a simple identity or similarity of motifs is not at all sufficient to establish the

literary motifs played a significant role in that epoch of the development of literary history when interest was payed principally to the question of "influences" and "borrowings": similarity of a motif was considered sufficient and indubitable proof that a later writer had "borrowed" this motif from another, chronologically earlier writer. Today literary historians attempt to see in a similarity of separate motifs proof only of "spiritual" or artistic affinity of writers making use of the same motifs in their works. This is also my point of view.

There have unfortunately been very few separate attempts at a systematic survey of the motifs of one or the other literary trend or of the motifs of an individual writer. For the further successful development of historico-literary research, such surveys, and even "dictionaries", indices of literary motifs, are absolutely indispensable. When this is done one important circumstance will undoubtedly become clear: literary motifs will be seen to fall into two principal groups. To the first belong "eternal" motifs, recurring in various stylistic epochs. [6] To the second belong motifs encountered only in certain epochs or even in one particular epoch only. Between these groups there is a transitional group: to it belong motifs which, it is true, recur in various epochs, but which vary greatly, take very different forms, or express totally different content. [7] We shall conditionally term motifs belonging to the first group "eternal", and those of the second group "temporary", adding to this designation the name of the corresponding literary epoch (a temporary baroque, classical, romantic motif, etc.). Motifs of the transitional group can be termed romantic, symbolist, etc., variations of eternal motifs. The term "eternal", of course, must be taken *cum grano salis*; the eternity of a motif and the universality of its diffusion are of course almost always limited:

---

influence of one author on another. It is much more important to establish the "spiritual kinship" or the mutual repulsion of authors. Several articles in my collections *Aus zwei Welten* ('s-Gravenhage, 1957) and *Russische Dichter* (forthcoming) are devoted to a series of eternal and temporary motifs of Slavic literatures.

[6]   *Cf.* especially R. R. Curtius, *Europäische Literatur und lateinisches Mittelalter* (Bern, 1948).

[7]   *Cf.* the second chapter of this article.

eternal motifs are sometimes not to be found even among kindred peoples; a number of eternal motifs of European literature are not met, for example, even in Indic literature, not to mention the literatures of the Far East; there, instead of these motifs, appear completely different ones, eternal from the point of view of Indic, Chinese, or Japanese literature. [8]

In what follows we shall deal with several eternal and temporary motifs of Slavic romantic literatures. I hope that even a cursory survey of them will give the reader a clear idea of their significance for the description of both the individual traits of Slavic romanticism and its affinity with other epochs in the history of Slavic literatures. – In connection with the analysis of motifs of Slavic romantic literatures we shall deal with certain questions touching upon literary stylistics, and vocabulary.

[8] An interesting analysis of individual motifs of Indic poetry is given by M. Kalynovyč, 'Priroda i byt v staroindijskoj drame', *Kievskie Universitetskie Izvestija*, LVI (1916), I, pp. 1–48, and separately (Kiev, 1916).

II

A NEW ATTITUDE TOWARD NATURE —
WATERFALLS

The romantic Weltanschauung brings a radical change in the attitude of man – and of the poet in particular – toward nature. Nature is no longer a mechanism, but a living organism. Furthermore, nature cannot be the object of purely mechanistic and mathematical investigation: she contains profundities, secrets, and supernatural or spiritual content. Precisely because of these features, going beyond the bounds of the machanistic view of the eighteenth-century Enlightenment, nature is contiguous with the profundities of the human being. This contiguity gives man the possibility of conscious, semi-conscious, and subconscious spiritual intercourse with nature.[1] This finds expression in the motif, constantly recurring in romantic poetry, of "conversation" with nature. Nature, however, is either mute, or speaks an "incomprehensible", "secret", or "silent" tongue. The sounds, the "voice", the "speech" of nature are incomprehensible directly to the poet; at least, they are incomprehensible to his intelligence. Therefore the poet's "conversation" with nature is in romantic poetry a monologue of the poet, directed to nature. Nature's "answer" is given by the poet himself, by means of a symbolic interpretation of nature's sounds, voices, or of some trait or phenomenon of hers.

The "nocturnal poems" of romantic poets have frequently been commented upon, especially those of Tjutčev,[2] but the "nocturnal

---

[1] See my *Outline . . .*, p. 87*f.*, and the collection of texts edited by Ch. Bernoulli and H. Kern, *Romantische Naturphilosophie* (Jena, 1926).

[2] My article 'Tjutčev und die deutsche Romantik', *ZfslPh.*, IV (1928), 3/4, pp. 299–323, review of the symposium *Urania* in *ZfslPh.*, VII (1931), 3/4, pp. 299–323, and my collection *Russische Dichter*.

11

poems" of Žukovskij, Lermontov, Fet, the Polish romanticists, K. H. Mácha, and even Puškin are undoubtedly closely connected with Tjutčev's "poetry of the night".[3]

Such is the relation of the romantic poets to the "elements"... Among poems dedicated to the elements, the many poems of Russian poets devoted to waterfalls are manifest. As is well known, there are very few waterfalls in Russia. Deržavin, while on official business, became acquainted with the Kivač, an unimportant waterfall, or rather rapid, in northern Russia. A pictorial and colorist poet, Deržavin made use of the picture of the waterfall as a landscape in his ode *The Waterfall*. Only the first verse of this long ode is actually devoted to the waterfall. This verse speaks only of the play of light and colors:

> Алмазна сыплется гора
> с высот четыремя скалами,
> жемчугу бездна и сребра
> кипит внизу, бьет вверх буграми.
> От брызгов синий холм стоит,
> далече рев в лесу гремит.

"The diamantine mountain falls from the heights over four cliffs, the abyss of pearl and silver boils beneath, springs up like hillocks. From the spray a deep-blue hill arises, far-off a roar in the forest thunders."

Deržavin does not forget the sounds of the waterfall, but he speaks only of the influence of its roar (*rev*) on animals: a wolf, a roe, a steed (stanzas 5-7); the waterfall, a natural phenomenon, and its voice are as it were directed only to nature... For man the waterfall is merely cause for reflection:

> не жизнь ли человеков нам
> сей водопад изображает? –
>
> .   .   .   .
>
> Не так ли с неба время льется,

[3] Interesting, for example, are the "nocturnal poems" of the Czech poet V. S. Nebeský (1818–82), which are in many ways harmonious with the poems of Tjutčev, although there is no genetic relation between the works of the two poets. A completely different type of "poetry of the night" appears in the German and Czech poems of K. H. Mácha.

кипит стремление страстей,
честь блещет, слава раздается,
мелькает счастье наших дней... (stanzas 10-11)

"Is it not the life of man this waterfall depicts for us? – Is it not thus that
time streams down from heaven, the striving of the passions seethes,
honor sparkles, fame resounds, the joy of our times flashes ..."

Thus Deržavin connects his favorite baroque theme, the "perishability and transitory character of all earthly existence", with
the waterfall. Only after lengthy meditation, at the end of the ode,
does Deržavin address the waterfall: here again, as in the first
verse, it is only an aesthetic image:

Шуми, шуми, о водопад!
. . . .
Увеселяй и слух и взгляд
твоим стремленьем светлым, звучным,
и в поздней памяти людей
живи лишь красотой твоей! (stanza 70)

"Sound, sound, o waterfall!... divert both ear and eye by thy bright
and sonorous streaming, live in man's later memory only by thy beauty!"

But imagination carries him off along the quiet river Suna, on
which lies the waterfall Kivač – and Deržavin bids the waterfall
farewell in lines that are again coloristic:

И ты, о водопадов мать,
река на севере гремяща,
о Суна! коль с высот блистать
ты можешь, и от зарь горяща
кипишь и сеешься дождем,
сафирным, пурпурным огнем. (stanza 72)

"And you, o mother of waterfalls, river thundering in the North, o
Suna! how from the heights you sparkle, and burning in the dawn you
boil and sprinkle like a rain in saphire purple fire."

Deržavin's friend V. Kapnist, in a poem dedicated to the memory
of Deržavin, varies Deržavin's description of the Kivač, calling

attention to *The Waterfall*, one of the most remarkable odes of his late friend:[4]

> . . . . . подобно водопаду,
> что с гор высоких вдаль стремит
> хрустальну быстрых вод громаду,
> и громом грома звук глушит,
> в алмазах солнца луч играет,
> и радугу изображает
> в поднявшейся от брызгов мгле; –
> жемчуг клубами в пене льется...

"...like a waterfall, that from the lofty peaks casts down the crystal mass of rapid waters and with thunder thunder's tongue makes mute, the sun's ray plays in diamonds, paints the rainbow in the mist arising from the spray; – in the foam flow clouds of pearl."

Kapnist completes this scene, in which Deržavin's imagery is also repeated (*bryzgi, almaz, žemčug, grom*), with a coloristic picture of the waterfall frozen in winter:

> Но вдруг зима, дохнувши мразом,
> падущи леденит ручьи:

[4] Henceforth I cite poets according to the latest editions; less well-known poets are cited with indication of place of publication and pages. – Kapnist, in the poem *Obuchovka* (1818, *i.e.* two years after the poem on Deržavin's death), utilizes the imagery of Deržavin's *Vodopad* in describing a water-mill. The description of waterfalls in Karamzin's *Pis'ma russkogo putešestvennika* utilizes almost exclusively words which denote optical (*serebrjanyj, belaja kipjaščaja pena, stolb mlečnoj peny, bryzgi, mlečnye oblaka vlažnoj pyli, pyl' ili tončajšij srebrjanyj dožd'*) or acoustic (*rev, šum*) impressions. Only in regard to the Rhine waterfall does he use expressions characterizing aesthetic experience: *prekrasnoe velikolepnoe zrelišče, veličavyj, neizglagolannyj* (*Sočinenija Karamzina*, vol. III, Moscow, 1920, pp. 66–8), and later writes of waterfalls in general *veličestvennye čudesa prirody* (p. 130). True, the Rhine waterfall evoked *sil'nye dviženija v duše* (p. 68), but he does not find it necessary to say just what sort of movements these were. In *Pis'ma* . . . (cited edition), Karamzin speaks of waterfalls on pp. 106 (a mountain stream), 115–116 (Staubbach), 119, 129 (Reichenbach). In the classicist tradition is the mention of waterfalls in the young N. Bobriščev-Puškin (1816, *Dovol'stvo i spokojstvie*, first in the collection *Kalliopa*, Moscow, 1817, reprinted in the collection edited by V. Orlov: *Dekabristy. Poezija, dramaturgija, proza* . . ., M.–L., 1951, p. 180), *rev, žemčužnaja rosa*, and in Žukovskij (1819, *Gosudaryne Imperatrice Marii Fedorovne*), *mlečnaja pena*.

блестящи яхонтом, алмазом,
оцепенев, висят струи;
по них сверкает луч игривый;
и разноцветные отливы
еще ярчее взор разят...

"But abruptly winter, breathing frost, freezes the falling streams: sparkling ruby and diamond, the torrents hang frozen; in them gleams a playful ray; variegated color-changes strike the eye still stronger..."

Karamzin's descriptions of waterfalls on the Rhine and in Switzerland are of the same character. [5]

But let a romanticist, Boratynskij, approach a waterfall, this time the Imatra in Finland. For him, the waterfall is like a living being, to whom he speaks (beginning, incidentally, with Deržavin's words):

Шуми, шуми с крутой вершины,
не умолкай, поток седой!
Соединяй протяжный вой
с протяжным отзывом долины!

. . . .

и с непогодою ревучей
твой рев мятежный соглашен.
    Зачем с безумным ожиданьем
к тебе прислушиваюсь я?
зачем трепещет грудь моя
каким-то вещим трепетаньем?
    Как очарованый стою
над дымной бездною твоею
и, мнится, сердцем разумею
речь безглагольную твою. (1821).

"Sound, sound from the steep summit, do not fall still, o grey torrent! Unite thy lengthy roar to the valley's lengthy echo...! and with the roaring storm thy stormy roar accords. Why do I listen to thee in senseless expectation? Why does my breast tremble with some prophetic trepidation? As if charmed, I stand above thy misty chasm and, it seems, with my heart I understand thy wordless speech."

[5]   Cf. note 4, p. 14.

This is already a "conversation" with the waterfall, an attempt to understand its wordless (*bezglagol'nuju*) "speech". And it is characteristic that the colorful visual picture of the waterfall has entirely disappeared!

In the same year another romanticist, Bestužev-Marlinskij, extolled the Narva-waterfall in a verse fragment included in a prose article. [6] Marlinskij joins new imagery and the "psychologization" of a natural phenomenon to the pictorial style of Deržavin and Kapnist: in "pearly crest" (*ožemčužennoj grjadoj*) the waves

> . . . прядая через скалы,
> играют в красоте чудесной
> отливом радуги небесной,
> огнями громовой стрелы;
> вот в бурные слились валы
> и с грохотом алмазну стену,
> упав, разбрызгивают в пену...

"...springing over the cliffs, the heavenly rainbow's colors play in their marvellous beauty, like the thunder-arrow's fires; here they flow together in stormy waves and, falling, with a roar explode the diamond wall in foam..."

the streams

> то брызжут золотым снопом,
> то гнутся радугою смелой,
> то, вспыхнувши цветным лучем,
> летят и гаснут в пене белой...

"now spurt into a golden sheaf, now bend into a daring rainbow, now, blazing in a colored ray, fly and fade in the white foam..."

Nor does Marlinskij forget the "frozen waterfall":

> и цепи мхов, и плющ печальной
> корой подернуты кристальной;
> гроздями вылился алмаз;
> с прибрежных сосн, с ветвей долины

[6] *Poezdka v Revel'*, 1821; cited according to the *Stichotvorenija* of Bestužev-Marlinskij in *Bol'šaja Biblioteka Poèta* (1948), pp. 126f. Other poems of Marlinskij *ibidem*.

кистями зыблются рубины
и блеском ослепляют глаз...

"And chains of moss, and the sad ivy covered with a crystal crust; the diamonds flow in clusters; from the pines of the shore, from the branches of the valley tassels of rubies tremble and blind the eye with their brilliance."

But for Marlinskij the waterfall's waves are already living beings:

толпятся волны за волною
в стесненный боязливый круг.
Вот близко пропасти... и вдруг,
сверкнув лучом хрустальной влаги,
вниз скачут, полные отваги...

Струи свергаясь пеленою,
как бы играют меж собою...

"wave after wave crowds together in a tight fearful circle. Here, close to the cliff... and suddenly, flashing a ray of crystal moisture, leap down, full of daring... The streams, falling like a curtain, play as if with one another..."

And Marlinskij, of course, does not forget his subjective impression:

все обольщенье уловляло
и все в мечтателе питало
души оптический обман.[7]

"All enchantment caught the dreamer and fed in him the optical illusion of the soul."

While admiring the waterfall, Marlinskij "remembers the misfortune of one of my forebears". "Slowly and with a heavy heart I drew away from the rapids, and the waterfall's distant sound awoke in my memory echoes of the distant and not-so-distant past." The objective symbol of Deržavin has been replaced by subjective reminiscence...

On a level with Boratynskij's poem stands the *The force of Song*

[7] Cf. "*optičeskij obman*" in the *Russkie Noči* of prince V. Odoevskij (re-edited Moscow, 1913), pp. 65, 87, and N. Polevoj, *Moskovskij Telegraf*, 1833, vol. II, p. 234.

(*Sila pesnopenija*) published in 1824 by the young poet S. Ševyrev;[8] formally an ode, but in theme and phraseology a purely romantic work, this poem joins to the lexical tradition of the eighteenth century the influences of the circle of "Ljubomudry" to which Ševyrev belonged. The first verse of this poem presents poetic creation in the image of a waterfall:

> Как бурный ток с утесов гордых
> стремится шумною волной,
> обломки скал вращает твердых
> и дубы рушит пред собой; –
> и смотрит путник изумленный
> на светлый пар летучей пены
> и слышит грозный рев волны:
> но он не зрит, отколь стремленья,
> так льются волны песнопенья
> из тайной сердца глубины.

"Like a stormy current from the proud cliffs it flows in noisy waves, tosses about the fragments of hard rock, destroys the oaks before it; – and the astounded wayfarer regards the light vapor of the flying foam and hears the wave's stern roar, but he does not see from where this rushing comes, thus flow the waves of singing from the secret depth of the heart."

Here the symbol of the waterfall, like the night and the wind in Tjutčev later, symbolizes that same "secret depth of the heart", a fundamental conception of romantic psychology. [9] In later poems Russian romanticists either cannot or will not lend such ponderous symbolism to the image of the waterfall as did Boratynskij and Ševyrev. But the image itself is preserved, one of those typical of Russian romanticism.

In the same year a waterfall appears in Kjuchel'beker's ode on the death of Byron: the poet is like a waterfall:

> Так водопад между скалами
> ревет, пугает взор и слух;

---

[8] In *Trudy Obščestva Ljubitelej Rossijskoj Slovesnosti*, V (Moscow, 1824), pp. 285ff. Not the collected poetry of Ševyrev in *Bol'šaja Biblioteka Poèta*.

[9] See my *Outline . . .*, pp. 86 and 87; further, Chapter 3 of this work and the remarks on the concept "heart" in Chapter 4.

ярясь, стремится в край надзвездный;
вдруг исчезает в мраке бездны...

"Thus a waterfall between the cliffs roars and frightens eye and ear; in fury, rushes to the space above the stars; abruptly disappears into the chasm's darkness..."

For Kjuchel'beker the waterfall is obviously a metaphor both of poetic creation and of the poet's ruin. The image of the poet's creativity as a waterfall is repeated briefly in 1834 (*Isfrail*, at the end: "*kak gornyj tok, iduščij v doly*"). But at approximately the same time (the 1830's), in the poem *Time* (*Vremja*), Kjuchel'beker returns to Deržavin's image of the waterfall-time, even repeating the Deržavin-like optical imagery:

с крутизны кипит жемчуг,
блеск и радуга вокруг...

"From the steep slope the pearls boil down, around all is brilliance and rainbow..."

The same image occurs in the poem *To My Brother* (*Bratu* 1833).

In 1826 the romantic theoretician prince P. Vjazemskij writes his *Waterfall* (once again the Narva waterfall gives rise to a poem). We meet echoes of Deržavin's imagery in Vjazemskij's work too, but for him the main thing is subjective experience and a no less subjective symbolic interpretation; visual images, incidentally, occupy a minimal place:

жемчужною, кипящей лавой...
дождь брызжет от упорной сшибки
волны...

и влажный дым, как облак зыбкий...

"like the pearly burning lava... spurts the rain from the stubborn impact of the wave... and the damp smoke, like an unsteady cloud."

The poem begins with an address to the waterfall:

Несись с неукротимым гневом,
мятежной влаги властелин!
Над тишиной окрестной ревом
господствуй, бурный исполин!

"Rush with indomitable anger, o master of rebellious water! Rule the surroundings silence with thy roar, o stormy giant!"

The "psychologization" of the waterfall is continued in what follows: the waterfall is a "struggle", a "battle", a "clash" (*bor'ba, boj, sšibka*) of "wave fighting with wave" (*volny srazivšejsja s volnoj*). To the "implacable anger" (*neukrotimomu gnevu*) of the waterfall is joined its "ferocity" (*svirepstvovanie*). A series of psychological epithets: "angry", "infuriated", "sullen" (*serdityj, razъjarennyj, ugrjumyj*), "internecine-stormy waves" (*meždousobno-burnye volny*), and the author speaks of himself:

> Я мыслью погружаюсь в шуме
> междоусобно-бурных волн.

"In thought I sink within the noise of the internecine-stormy waves."

The central thought of the poem is an antithesis between the waterfall and the calm beauty of nature, but it is the "insurgent" waterfall that is close to the soul of man. The poem concludes with a philosophic interpretation, recalling in character (but not in strength of poetic expression) the poetry of Tjutčev:

> Противоречие природы,
> под грозным знаменем тревог,
> в залоге вечной непогоды
> ты бытия приял залог.
> Ворвавшись в сей предел спокойный,
> один свирепствуешь в глуши,
> как вдоль пустыни вихорь знойный,
> как страсть в святилище души.
> Как ты, внезапно разразится,
> как ты, растет она в борьбе,
> терзает лоно, где родится,
> и поглощается в себе.

"Contradiction of nature, beneath the stern banner of unrest, as a pawn of eternal bad weather you received the pledge of existence. Bursting upon this calm province, you rule alone in the silence, as the fiery whirlwind in the desert, as a passion in the temple of the soul. Like you, it breaks out suddenly, like you, it grows in struggle, rends the womb that bears it, and is in itself devoured."

It is interesting that in Vjazemskij's romantic *Waterfall* there are still very noticeable elements of classicist vocabulary: *svjatilišče, igrališče, zercalo, prijal, sej, votšče*, etc. Nevertheless the poem's artistic resources are deliberately romantic: apart from the "psychological epithets", we notice, precisely in a traditionally Deržavin-like colorist line, a paradoxical rapprochement of water and fire: the water is "lava". [11]

In 1829 (written in 1827–8) appears Fedor Glinka's *Karelija*, in which we find a picture of Deržavin's Kivač. The transposition of Deržavin's stanza into iambic tetrameter is framed by a sonorous and subjective tableau:

> Но что шумит?... В пустыне шопот
> растет, растет, звучит и вдруг –
> как будто конной рати топот
> дивит и ужасает слух!

"What noise is that?... in the wilderness a whisper grows, grows, sounds and suddenly – like the trample of a mounted host amazes and aws the hearing!"

but here there is also an address to the waterfall:

> "Кивач! Кивач!... Ответствуй, ты ли?"
> И выслал бурю он в ответ.

"Kivač! Kivač!... Answer, is it thou? And he sent a storm in answer."

The coloristic tableau, incidentally, is somewhat changed by the personification of the waterfall: "mighty giant" (*mogučij ispolin*), complemented by a picture of the waterfall at night, and completed by a lyric ending:

> Тут буду я! Тут жизнь теки!
> О счастье жизни сей волнистой!
> Где ты? – В чертоге ль богача,
> в обетах роскоши нечистой,
> или в Карелии лесистой,
> под вечным шумом Кивача?

---

[11] Paradoxical rapprochements are characteristic of the romantic style, *cf.* the remarks in my commentary to *Evgenij Onegin* (Cambridge, Mass., 1953), p. 257 *et al.*

"Here I shall be! Here shall my life flow by! O joy of this life of waves! Where art thou? In the chambers of the rich, in the lures of unclean luxury, or in wooded Carelia, by the eternal sound of the Kivač?"

The Decembrist poets became familiar with the mountain rivers and streams of Siberia, and turn to them with the same lyric monologues. In 1828 Bestužev-Marlinskij sings of the waterfall Šebutuj:

> Стенай, шуми, поток пустынной,
> неизмеримый Шебутуй...

"Groan, sound, wilderness stream, immeasurable Šebutuj..."

And the image of the Siberian waterfall now unites both personification and subjectively lyric motifs:

> Катись под роковою силой,
> неукротимый Шебутуй!
> Твое роптанье – голос милой,
> твой ливень – братский поцелуй!
>
> Когда громам твоим внимаю
> и в кудри льется брызгов пыль –
> невольно я припоминаю
> свою таинственную быль...
>
> Тебе подобно, гордый, шумной,
> от высоты родимых скал
> влекомый страстию безумной,
> я в бездну гибели упал!...

"Flow beneath the fatal force of the implacable Šebutuj! Thy grumbling is the beloved's voice, thy shower a brotherly kiss! When I hear thy thunder and the dust of thy raindrops wets my hair – involuntarily I remember my own clandestine past... Like you, proud, noisy I fell, drawn by a mad passion, from the heights of native cliffs into the abyss of ruin!..."

The process of remaking the imagery, of the "subjectivization" of the poem's content, and of the personification of the images of nature, continually pushes the visual imagery into the background and brings to the fore impressions of sound, symbolizing the "voice" of the waterfall for the romantic poets. It is characteristic that Marlinskij strikes out from his poem to the Šebutuj the pictorial stanza:

> и над тобой краса природы;
> полувоздушный перлов мост
> сгибает радужные своды,
> блестя, как райской птицы хвост...

"And above thee nature's beauty; the half-airy bridge of pearls bends its rainbow arches, brilliant as a bird-of-paradise' taill..."

In the following year, 1829, Marlinskij writes the reminiscent poem *Finland*. Here there is only a relic of a pictorial image:

> . . . с крутизны в пустынные заливы,
> как радуги, бегут ключи игривы.

"From the heights into deserted bays the playful streams like rainbows run."

But the image of Finnish waterfalls is already purely sonorous; not without romantic lexical allusions (revolution is a "tocsin" [*nabat*]; hell):

> Там силой вод пробитые громады
> задвинули порогом пенный ад,
> и в бездну их крутятся водопады,
> гремучие, как воющий набат;
> им вторит гул – жилец пещеры дальней,
> как тяжкий млат по адской наковальне...

"There the rocky masses, pierced by the waters' force, close off in rapids the foamy hell, and in their chasm spin waterfalls, howling like the wailing tocsin; they are answered by a rumble, tenant of a distant grotto, like a heavy hammer on the hellish anvil."

The poem ends in lines in which all nature is but a symbol: for the poet, traces of surf on the cliffs are "runes" – "I understood them" –

> и с древних гор заветные скрижали
> мне дивные пророчества роптали!

"And from the ancient mountains the sacred tablets whispered marvellous prophecies to me!"

In 1830 N. M. Jazykov uses the image of a waterfall, this time the Niagara, to present the eternal motif of the drowning swimmer[12] in a new light. In his picture of the waterfall sound elements are moved to the fore. Furthermore the image of the waterfall itself (the first and last – fourth – stanzas of the poem) is unclear:

> Море бреска, гул, удары,
> и земля потрясена;
> то стеклянная стена
> о скалы раздроблена,
> то бегут чрез крутояры
> многоводной Ниагары
> ширина и глубина!

"A sea of glitter, rumbling, blows, and the earth is shaken; there is a wall of glass broken against the cliffs, there the width and depth of water-laden Niagara flee over the steep descent!"

In 1832 (written in 1830 or '31) appears Poležaev's poem *The Waterfall*. In it, too, only an insignificant role is played by pictorial images:

> Громады волн буграми хлещут
> в паденьи быстром и крутом

---

[12] The image of the drowning swimmer is common in baroque poetry; see my book *Filosofija H. S. Skovorody* (Warsaw, 1934), pp. 196, 202 note 20. In Russian romantic poetry we find it in Žukovskij (*Plovec*, 1811), Kozlov (*K drugu Žukovskomu*, 1822; *Plovec*, 1823; *Novye stansy*, 1827; *Burja*, 1828; *Dva čelnoka*, 1833; *Razluka*, 1836), Poležaev (*Pesn' pogibajuščego plovca*, 1828), Jazykov (in three poems with the same title *Plovec* before 1829, 1831, and 1839), prince Vjazemskij (at the end of the poem *Volnenie*, 1829), Lermontov (*Groza šumit . . .*, 1830; *Romans*, 1831; *Želanie*, stanza 2, 1832), Denis Davydov (*I moja zvezdočka*, 1834), A. Timofeev (*Razluka*, before 1835), N. Ogarev (*Christianin*, 1838), and many other Russian poets. In other Slavic literatures one should note expecially the poems of Mickiewicz *Żeglarz* (*O morze zjawisk*) (1821), with echoes of baroque symbolism of the sea, *W imionniku K. R.* and *Żeglarz* (*Z imionnika Z.*) (both 1825), and the 3d and 4th *Crimean Sonnets*; in Czech romanticism, Mách's *Dítě* (see the edition of Fr. Krčma, K. H. Mácha, *Dílo*, Prague, 1928, vol. I, 127) and K. Sabina's *Na plavbe* (1835); in the Jugoslav, the poems of Stanko Vraz *Vrpca* and *Srce* (both printed in 1845). This image is symbolically applied in V. Tumanskij's *Elegija* (1824) and *Setovanie* (1825), in the *Sočinenija* of Tumanskij edited by S. Brailovskij (SPb, 1912), pp. 137ff. and 150ff.

24

> и, разлетевшись, ярко блещут
> вокруг серебряным дождем.

"The wave-masses strike like hillocks in their steep and rapid fall and, flying apart, gleam clearly brilliant, like a silver rain."

Sound is in the forefront:

> Ревет и стонет гул протяжной
> по разорвавшейся реке
> и, исчезая с пеной влажной,
> смолкает глухо вдалеке.

"The drawn-out rumble howls and groans along the exploded river and, disappearing in moist foam, grows mutely silent in the distance."

And psychological symbolism is the fundamental theme of the second half of the poem:

> Вот наша жизнь! вот образ верной
> погибшей юности моей! –
> она в красе нелицемерной
> сперва катилась, как ручей;
> потом в пылу страстей безумных,
> быстра, как горный водопад,
> исчезла вдруг при плесках шумных,
> как эха дальнего раскат.

"Here is our life! here the true image of my lost youth! – it flowed at first in its true beauty, like a brook; then in the heat of senseless passions rapid, like a mountain waterfall, it disappeared abruptly in loud splashings, like a distant echo's peal."

And again an appeal to the waterfall, which is here a symbol not only of the passions, but also of freedom:

> Шуми, шуми, о сын природы!
> Ты безотрадною порой
> певцу напомнил блеск свободы
> своей свободною игрой!

"Sound, sound, o son of nature! In a cheerless time you recalled to the bard in your free play the glint of freedom!"

25

Again in 1840, V. Raevskij, banished to Siberia in 1827, addresses a mountain stream with the exotic name Ikaguan:

> Шумн, шуми, Икагуан,
> твой шум глухой, однообразный
> слился в одно с толпою дум
> с мечтой печальной и бессвязной!

"Sound, sound, Ikaguan, your toneless, monotonous sound has flowed together with a host of thoughts, with a sad and incoherent dream!

The mountain torrent is a symbol of aspiration toward freedom:

> Внизу шумит Икагуан,
> ревут его в утесах воды...
> Зачем они кипят струей,
> куда, белея пеной снежной,
> как бурей взломанной стезей,
> несут свой шум, разбег мятежный?
> Спроси природу, где устав
> для сил надменных и свободы?
> Они не знают наших прав, –
> здесь горы, каменные своды
> и зимний лед их волю жмут.
> С вершины горного Саяна
> они летят, они бегут
> к бретам привольным океана...

"The Ikaguan sounds below, his waters roar between the cliffs ... Why do they boil in torrent, whereto, white in snowy foam, as if along a stormy run? Ask nature, where is the law for her haughty forces and her freedom? They do not know our laws, – here mountains, stony vaults and winter ice restrain their freedom. From the heights of the mountainous Sajan they fly, they flow to the ocean's untrammelled shores..."

And, as it seems, the last poem devoted to waterfalls and mountain streams is the *Argun'* of Kjuchel'beker (1842); this is already a purely lyric poem about one of the rivers which the poet, a "wanderer" (*skitalec*), had "visited", and, as in other cases, he says good-by on the riverbank to his "last friend" (the Polish exile K. Sawiczewski). Only the title of the poem *Argun'* and one line,

Шуми же, о Аргунь, мое благословенье!

"Announce my blessing, o Argun!"

show that this waterfall is for Kjuchel'beker an image of the eternal anxiety in the poet's soul and of the continual loss of his friends.[13]

A remarkable example of the "psychologization" of the waterfall image is found in a poem written before 1836 by the Czech romantic K. H. Mácha: a mountain torrent and waterfall rushes off somewhere, toward the poet's distant and unknown beloved (la *princesse lointaine*):

> Umlkni, potoku hlučný,
> padající z kolmých skal...
>
> .   .   .   .
>
> O čem mluvíš? O jen o ní!
> Kde jest ona? Rci kde dlí?
> V lůno její jen se kloní
> rychlý běh tvůj? K ní, jen k ní?
> Proč mě touha po ní moří?
> Tváří jejích neviděl jsem,
> hlasů jejích neslyšel jsem,
> předce mé srdce láskou hoří.
> O čem mluvíš? o jen o ní!
> Rci! Proč pláčeš? o jen pro ní!

[13] Waterfall images are found in Puškin in the poems *Kavkaz* and *Terek* (both 1829); the Terek is depicted as a wild beast, as is the sea in *Mednyj Vsadnik* (*cf.* chapter 3, note 33). Lermontov mentions waterfalls and mountain streams in poems, but all his Caucasian scenes take on symbolic meaning only in the context (see *Mcyri*, stanza 10; *Izmail Bej*, stanzas I, 21, II, 1, and III, 27; *Chadži Abrek*, beginning). Waterfalls are only mentioned by Kozlov (*Drugu Žukovskomu*, 1822; *Stansy Gnediču*, 1825), and Kjuchel'beker (*Svjatopolk*, part III, 1824; *Edinoborstvo Gomera i Davida*, post 1829; *Bratu*, 1833 – citations from the *Stichotvorenija* of Kjuchel'beker in *Bol'šaja Biblioteka Poèta*, vol. I, 1839, pp. 99, 109, 148, *cf.* also 150), by V. Tepljakov (1804–42) in the poem *Kavkaz* (before 1832?), where waterfalls "*serebrom rastoplennym letjat*" (*cf.* N. Gerbel', *Russkie poèty*, 2nd ed., 1888, p. 275). The theme of P. Eršov's *Dream* (1834) is original: this is a waterfall that the poet sees in a dream. In Słovacki, together with a waterfall scene in the poem *W Szwajcarii. I* (before 1839), there is an interesting symbolic image of the waterfall-soul in *Do pani Joanny Bobrowej* (1845).

"Fall still, sonorous stream, falling from steep cliffs?... Of what speak you? Only of her! Where is she? Say, where? Bends your swift course to her bosom? To her, to her alone? Why does this yearning for her overcome me? I have not seen her face, I have not heard her voice, and yet my heart burns with love. Of what speak you? Only of her! Say! Why weep you? Only for her!"

Mickiewicz has a remarkable fragment, beginning with the words:

Wsłuchac się w szum wód głuchy, zimny i jednaki
i przez fale rozeznać myśl wód jak przez znaki...

"To heed the muffled, cold, monotonous sound of waters and recognize in the waves the waters' thought, as if by omens..."

However, it is a question here of the element water in general, of the river or the sea... Nevertheless, these lines express clearly the new theme of romantic poetry of nature. It is worthwhile to remember as well Kjuchel'beker's words, addressed to the wind (*The Wind*, 1827 or '28):

Пусть леса, холмы и долы
огласит твой шумный зык!
Внятны мне твои глаголы,
мне понятен твой язык.

"Let thy sonorous cry fill woods, hills, and valleys! To me thy words are clear, to me thy tongue is plain."

III

VOCABULARY — REINTERPRETATION — NEOLOGISMS

It is not difficult to notice that all Russian poem devoted to water-falls and mountain streams display a considerable unity of vocabulary. However, the repetition of words and of images connected with them divides the vocabulary of waterfall poems into two groups. To the first belong visual, coloristic designations: diamonds–*almazy* (or *almaznyj*) in Deržavin, Kapnist, Bestužev-Marlinskij; pearls–*žemčug* in Deržavin, Kapnist, Vjazemskij, N. Bobriščev-Puškin, Glinka; other precious stones in Deržavin, Kapnist, Marlinskij; silver–*serebro* in Deržavin, Glinka, Poželaev; rainbow–*raduga* in Kapnist and Bestužev-Marlinskij. Other poets pay no attention to bright colors – which are undoubtedly really the most characteristic feature of the waterfall image. In certain poets we find non-coloristic visual images: foam–*pena*, smoke–*dym*, cloud–*oblako* (*i.e.*, little splashes of water).

On the other hand, the poets almost without exception mention the "roar", "thunder", "howl" (*rev, grom, voj*) of waterfalls and mountain torrents. In particular, Deržavin's address to the water-fall: "Sound, sound" (*Šumi, šumi*) is repeated by Boratynskij, Poležaev, and V. Raevskij, varied in Marlinskij's address to the Šebutuj: "Groan, sound" (*Stenaj, šumi*), and simplified be Kjuchel'-beker to "Sound, Argun'" (*Šumi že, o Argun'*). We meet different appeals to the waterfall in Vjazemskij: "Rush with implacable anger" (*Nesis' s neukrotimym gnevom*) and Glinka: "Kivač! Kivač! ... Answer..." (*Kivač Kivač!... Otvetstvuj...*).

In the Russian romantic poets we find a whole complex of words, known to us from Russian romantic poetry and connected with its fundamental ideological tendencies.[1] These words can be consolidated into specific semantic fields.[2] We encounter first of all a series of words connected with a change of judgments and appraisals in the sphere of man's spiritual life. Words of this semantic field are employed partially in the personification of the waterfall, which is presented as a living being, and partly in the portrayal of the poets' experience while contemplating the waterfall. All of these words are not new; we can find almost all of them in eighteenth-century poetry and prose, but they are "re-interpreted" and re-evaluated by the romanticists. Words with a negative, pejorative meaning began to be used in a positive sense; certain words acquired a completely new meaning;[3] others are simply characteristic of romanticism and manifest little or no semantic change. It is interesting that in the poems we have examined these words are encountered frequently and at times, so to say, in "contracted" form within a restricted context.

To the psychological words belongs first of all "mad", "insane" (*bezumnyj*) (in Boratynskij, Marlinskij, and Poležaev): Boratynskij listens to the waterfall's "speech" with "mad expectation" (*bezumnym ožidan'em*); both Marlinskij and Poležaev speak of the "insensate passion" (*bezymnych strastjach*) which has led them into an "abyss of ruin" (*bezdnu gibeli*). In no case, of course, can there be a question of a negative attitude on the poets' part toward their own experiences: neither poet was in the least disappointed in his revolutionary Weltanschauung. The romantic world-view in general uncovers a certain positive character in "madness"; romantic literature in the West and among the Slavs contains a series of "Apologies of Madness", proofs that in spiritual life the abnormal reveals certain spheres of cognition which are inaccessible to the normal person; in other cases the word *bezumnyj* signifies complete candour, spontaneity, and intensity of the feelings,

---

[1]   There are a few words on this subject in my commentary to *Evgenij Onegin*, Introduction, pp. xx–xxiv.

[2]   On this concept see Jost Trier, *Der deutsche Wortschatz im Sinnblick des Verstandes; die Geschichte eines sprachlichen Feldes* (Heidelberg, 1931).

[3]   See above note 1.

[4]   See Chapter 4.

passions (*strastej*) experienced.[4] The symbolic meaning of the waterfall image in the poems of Marlinskij and Poležaev shows that both poets see a certain "madness" of nature in the waterfall itself; we find analogous motifs in Vjazemskij's poem: the waterfall, a "contradiction of nature" (*protivorečie prirody*), is compared to passion, to the "fiery whirlwind" (*znojnym vichrem*).[5]

Boratynskij's "madness" is that he expects from the waterfall an answer to certain questions, the "marvellous prophecies" (*divnye proročestva*) of Marlinskij, the "blessing" (*blagoslovenie*) of Kjuchel'beker, understanding of the "wordless speech", of the "tongue" of nature. It seems to him (*mnitsja*) that he understands the waterfall's "speech". One can confront the word *mnitsja* with a series of words treating the poets' experience as a poetic illusion, effectively termed by Marlinskij an "optical illusion of the soul". The word "deception" (*obman*) itself was reinterpreted, principally by Puškin, as a designation of aesthetic illusion.[6] Apart from the word *obman*, one should notice Raevskij's "dream" (*mečta*), Boratynskij's *očarovannyj* (originally "bewitched"), and Marlinskij's "delusion" (*obol'ščenie*). All of these words, from various sides, help elucidate the conception of poetry as on the one hand "magic" (*volšebstvo*) and on the other "poetic illusion", the essence of aesthetic perception. Illusion (*der schöne Trug* of German aesthetics) is in a certain sense genuine cognition and a real force, the attitude towards which, of course, is not the same as that of the eighteenth-century Enlightenment. Puškin for this very reason defined *obman* more closely, as a poetic illusion, with the words "deception elevating us" (*nas vozvyšajuščij obman*).[7]

---

[5]   The word *strast'* in the sense of "passion", German "*Leidenschaft*", has a positive coloration in romantic poetry; in eighteenth-century psychology, on the other hand, a big role was played by the question of the "fight against the passions", undoubtedly under the influence of the Stoics (also in Descartes and Spinoza). Against "stoicism" see the remark of prince Vjazemskij (*Sočinenija*, vol. IX, 1884, *Staraja zapiasnja knižka*, p. 19, a remark of the late twenties). The word *strast'* had a pejorative meaning even later, among the realists (*cf.* Gončarov's *Oblomov*, part II, chapter II).

[6]   See my commentary to *Evgenij Onegin*, p. xxii.

[7]   See my articles 'Puškin und die Romantik', *Slavische Rundschau*, 1937, 2, pp. 69–80; *Germanoslavica*, V (1937–9), 1, pp. 1–31; 'Puškin medzi romantizmom a klasicizmom'. *Slovanské Pohl'ady*, 1937, 1, pp. 36–41, and 2, pp. 75–83.

Aesthetic perception is approached from another angle by words which point out something enigmatic, something beyond the bounds of the ordinary, in life and nature: poetic creation itself is connected with the "secret" depths of experience (Ševyrev), and man's life with its reversals is a "secret fact" (*tainstvennaja byl'*) (Marlinskij). Both words border upon the semantic field of enchanted (*očarovannyj*) and delusion (*obol'ščenie*).

Another semantic field, of words signifying mobility, changeability, or restlessness, is connected with the idea of man's subjective experiences. These words too are applied partly to the poets' experiences, partly to the waterfall, "personified", as we know, and presented as a living being. These words were reinterpreted and acquired a positive coloration. Such is, first of all, the word *mjatežnyj*, originally meaning "revolutionary", but signifying in the romantic lexicon precisely that side of spiritual experiences, their dynamism, which was presented as a symptom of their sincerity and depth. We find this word in Boratynskij (the waterfall's "rebellious roar" [*rev mjatežnyj*] is perhaps close to the "tocsin" [*nabat*] of Bestužev-Marlinskij), in Vjazemskij, who speaks of the waterfall's "insurgent moisture" (*mjatežnoj vlagi*), and in Raevskij (the "restless running" [*mjatežnyj razbeg*] of the waters of the Ikaguan). Close to this word are Boratynskij's "trembles" (*trepeščet*) and "trepidation" (*trepetan'e*) and Vjazemskij's "alarm" (*trevoga*). Spiritual experiences can be traced back to man's "heart" (*serdce*): Boratynskij "understands in [his] heart" (*serdcem razumeet*) the "wordless speech" of nature, and in Ševyrev's opinion poetic creativity originates in the "secret depth of the heart" (*iz tajnoj serdca glubiny*). The word *serdce* in the psychological sense is of course not new; in the romantic lexicon it loses a considerable portion of its emotional and sentimental coloration: both cases of the use of the word *serdce* in the poems mentioned testify with sufficient clarity to the fact that the "heart" is a symbolic designation of both the source of cognition and the source of creativity. Such is the meaning of this word, for example, in Tjutčev, who invests the heart (*Silentium*) not with feeling or emotion, but with "thought" (*mysl'*):

Как сердцу высказать себя?

. . . .

Мысль изреченная есть ложь...

"How can the heart express itself?... Thought expressed is falsehood."

As in Boratynskij, nature (*vetr nočnoj*") speaks a "language" "intelligible to the heart" (*jazykom ponjatnym serdcu*). This re-interpretation of the word *serdce* has a long tradition in Slavic romanticism. [8] The word "depth" (*glubina*), which is in addition "secret" (*tajnaja*), is particularly characteristic of the poetry of Ševyrev, serving as a constant symbol of that more profound side of spiritual life which romanticism opposes to the clear and transparent side of the soul, the intelligence. [9] The expression "depth" (*glubina*), applied to spiritual life, becomes current coin in the poetry of Russian romanticism. The very combination of words "in the depth of the heart", "in the depth of the soul" (*v glubine serdca, duši*), is now used even in everyday speech; it is possible that it was already used in the eighteenth century. [10] Thus Žukovskij has "in the depth of holy hearts" (*vo glubine svjatych serdec Dobrodetel'*, 2nd redaction, 1798) and "*v glubine duši*" (*Pis'mo k ****, 1814). But in the poetry of the romanticists it is changed into "heart-depth", "soul-depth" (*serdečnaja, duševnaja glubina*) and reinterpreted by the adjunction of images characterizing this "depth" as the place of birth and development of particularly significant feelings ("rapture", "inspiration" [*vostorg, vdochnove-nie*]) or thoughts. Kjuchel'beker, who in one of his early poems used the expression "the speechless depth of the soul" (*bezmolvnaja glubina duši*), like Žukovskij, in a completely neutral sense (*K samomu sebe*, 1818), already knows in 1834 that the "heart's depth" is the "eternal" source of poetic inspiration:

[8]   On the concept of the heart see P. Jurkevyč, 'Serdce i ego značenie v duchovnoj žizni čeloveka po učeniju slova Božija', *Trudy Kievskoj Duchovnoj Akademii*, 1860, I; on the views of Jurkevyč my *Narysy z istoriji filosofiji na Ukrajini* (Prague, 1931), pp. 150–152; B. Vyšeslavcev, *Serdce v christianskoj i indijskoj mistike* (Paris, 1929). See also chapter 4, note 48.
[9]   These words are taken from poems quoted in the preceding chapter.
[10]   *Glubina serdca* – *Hypatius-Chronicle*, ed. 1871, pp. 247, 412; *glubina serdečnaja* – ibidem, p. 399.

> . . .из сердечной глубины
> текут одни и те же звуки
> и вторятся из века в век. (Исфраил)

"From the heart's depth always the same sounds flow and are eternally repeated."

Also Puškin, *Derevnja* (*The Village*, 1819, *Sočinenija*, 1950, I, p. 352). N. Jazykov preserves the usual combination, reinterpreting it by the context:

> как волновалась во мне,
> на самой сердца глубине
> восторгов пламенная удаль. . ("Пушкину", 1826)

"As the fiery daring of delight surged in me, in the heart's very depth. . ."

> и поэтическая сила
> огнем могущественным била
> из глубины души моей ("А. М. Языкову", 1828)

"And poetic force sprang in puissant fire from the depth of my soul."

The expression *serdečnaja glubina* is used by Puškin in 1823 in the fragment "*I implored thee lately*" (*Ja umoljal tebja nedavno*) and the poem *Kn. M. A. Golicynoj* (both printed later), by D. Venevitinov in *To a Lover of Music* (*K ljubitelju muzyki*, 1826–7):

> . . . . . восторг свободный
> горит в сердечной глубине.

"Untrammelled rapture burns in the heart's depth."

and several times by Vjazemskij:

> . . . на тайном дне,
> в сердечной светлой глубине

"In the secret deep, in the heart's clear depth."

(*Progulka v stepi*, 1831), and especially in the poem *Salovka* (1829), the vocabulary of which is in general characteristic of romanticism:

> . . . природы вечно-новой
> небезглагольные черты
> в тебе внезапно пробуждают

пророчеств и преданий сны,
и волны тайных дум скликают
со дна сердечной глубины.

"The non-mute traits of nature ever new abruptly wake in you the
dreams of prophecy and legend, and call forth the waves of secret thought
from the bottom of the heart's depth."

(*cf.* also *Otryvki*.6, 1833; *Soznanie*, 1854). We find *duševnaja
glubina* in Tjutčev's *K.N.* (1824):

как жизни ключ, в душевой глубине

"Like life's source, in the soul's depths."

and *Silentium* (1830), and in Venevitinov's *Consolation* (*Ute-
šenie*, 1826); in the "soul-depth" there lives a "spark of noble
passion" (*iskra strasti blagorodnoj*). Tjutčev prefers the word
"abyss" (*bezdna*), which is very frequent in his works (applied
to the soul, for example, in *Holy night on the horizon has arisen*
(*Svjataja noč' na nebosklon vzošla*, 1850); the poet's soul is "amidst
the double drasm" (*meždu dvojnoju bezdnoj*, in *Lebed'*, 1839), or
"elements", "chaos" (*stichija, chaos*). These word combinations
are also found later in their new meaning, for example in an epigon
of romanticism, A. K. Tolstoj (*Est' mnogo zvukov v serdca glubine*,
1859).

A series of other epithets, aside from the *mjatežnyj* already
mentioned, are applied to the waterfall and its waters: "proud"
(*gordyj*), "implacable" (*neukrotimyj*), "menacing" (*groznyj*), "turbulent" (*bujnyj*), "stormy" and "storm" (*burnyj, burja*) "angry"
(*serdityj*), "savage" (*dikij*), "infuriated" (*razъjarennyj*), "gloomy"
(*ugrjumyj*), waves "full of daring" (*polnye otvagi*), and, as if in
contrast to these epithets, the words "play", "to play" (*igra, igrat'*).
These words, which are of course not new and not reinterpreted,
express a conception of the elements as "dynamically exalted"
(*das dynamisch Erhabene*). Vjazemskij found for the waterfall the
apt symbol "ruler" (*vlastelin*) and the epithet "majestic" (*veličavyj*),
in which are joined elements of the "exalted". Only the words
"implacable, stormy" (*neukrotimyj, bujnyj*), and "noisy" (*šumnyj*
as a human characteristic) are to a certain degree reinterpreted;

they are here imbued with a definitely positive coloration, although it is also possible to understand them in a negative sense.[11]

However, more essential are those words which connect the waterfall image with the notion of a force breaking out of a narrow frame, toward freedom, words connected with the idea of struggle, rebellion, or war: only Poležaev and Raevskij speak of "freedom" (*svoboda*), but to a certain degree, of course, both the word *mjatež-nyj* (*cf.* above) and Marlinskij's "tocsin", "grumble", "grumbling" (*nabat, ropot, roptan'e*) are connected with the idea of a popular uprising; the idea of battle is clear in Glinka's words "as the trampling of a mounted host" (*kak budto konnoj rati topot*) and Vjazemskij's "struggle", "battle", "collision", and "war" (*bor'ba, boj, sšibka, vojna*). The subjective aspect of the symbol of struggle and freedom is brought out (particularly by Vjazemskij) in the image of the "passions" (*strasti*), already occurring in Deržavin. It is interesting, however, that Deržavin's fundamental symbol, "time" and "perishability" (*vremja, tlennost'*) of all existence, is completely forgotten: this theme, typical of baroque poetry, is not unknown among the romanticists, but its absence probably demonstrates that the waterfall was a symbol precisely of a struggle in which there is hope of victory. Only in Vjazemskij are there echoes of the symbolism of the transitory character of existence, of "passion" (*i pogloščaetsja v sebe*), and Kjuchel'beker connects the mountain river with remembrance of parting with friends, with the transitory nature of friendship.

There is very little of romantic "natural philosophy" in romantic waterfall poetry. It is recalled only by Boratynskij's poem with its characterization of the waterfall as an "abyss" (*bezdna*) and its reminder of the waterfall's "wordless speech" (*bezglagol'naja reč'*). The "abyss" (and the "elements" [*stichija*] related to it) is very frequent in the romantic poets, for example in Tjutčev's poetry of the night; both Kjuchel'beker (quoted above) and Tjutčev (*cf.* above) speak of nature's language (of the wind); the same idea resounds in the last line of Puškin's "Night" (*Noč'*): "I search for

[11] The question of the re-evalution of word meanings is worthy of particular scrutiny: very often, a word's positive or negative coloration can only be determined by analysis of the context in which the word is used.

36

meaning in thee" (*Smysla ja v tebe išču*); this illegibly-written line was first "reconstructed" by Žukovskij – characteristically for him, for the romantic side of his poetry – as "I learn thy obscure tongue" (*temnyj tvoj jazyk uču*). And in any case, the waterfall image is approximated to a living being by that "fatal force" (*rokovaja sila*) which attracts the waves of the Šebuluj. There is no clear image of the water element as a wild beast: this image is repeated several times by Puškin – the Terek

> играет в свирепом весельи . . .
> играет и воет, как зверь молодой ("Кавказ", 1829)
>
> как зверь живой, ревет и воет
> ("Меж горных стен. . .", 1829)

"plays in truculent gaity; plays and howls, like a young animal; roars and howls, like a live animal."

and in the *Bronze Horseman* (1833):

> Нева вздувалась и ревела,
> котлом клокоча и клубясь,
> и вдруг, как зверь остервенясь,
> на город кинулась. . .[12]

"The Neva swelled and roared, like a cauldron cooking, swirling, and abruptly, like a frenzied beast, it rushed upon the city."

Later, the waters of the Neva, receding back into the riverbed, are compared to bandits. Marlinskij compares the implacable rush of the elements with "hell" (*ad*); the noise of the waterfall is "like a heavy hammer on hell's anvil" (*kak tjažkij mlat po adskoj nakoval'ne*); Vjazemskij calls the waters of the waterfall "boiling lava" (*kipjaščaja lava*), reminding the reader by this paradoxical comparison of a volcanic eruption – also one of the themes characteristic of romantic poetry.

The reinterpretation of words and their emotional re-evaluation is one of the most vital means by which a literary language develops,

[12]   G. Glebov, 'Filosofija prirody Puškina', *Puškinskij Vremennik*, II (1936), pp. 183–212, and my book *Gegel' v Rossii* (Paris, 1939), pp. 44–45.

but to this means comparatively little attention has been paid by investigators.

The manners of word reinterpretation are varied, but a principal role therein is played by the use of words in such a context that their new meaning and new emotional coloration leap to the reader's eye. One of the clearest cases of word reinterpretation is found in Puškin's "sounds" (*zvuki*) in the sense of poetry, verse;[13] "sleep" (*son*) in the sense of a spiritual experience beyond the reach of the ordinary, the everyday-poetic inspiration, dreaming, love, passion in general;[14] "deception" (*obman*) in the sense of aesthetic illusion.[15] In our lexical survey we saw the romanticists' reinterpretation of the words *mjatežnyj, trepetnyj, bezumnyj*. Particularly important is the re-evaluation of words: among those mentioned, the re-evaluation of "deception" (*obman*) and "folly" (*bezumie, bezumnyj*) is especially noteworthy. Both words, which were almost abusive, take on a positive coloration in the work of Puškin (and his contemporaries). *Obman* characterizes the force of an aesthetic impression (in *Evgenij Onegin* the "seductive deception [*obol'-stitel'nyj obman*] applied to pre-romantic literature, appraised favorably both by Puškin and by his readers – III, 9). *Bezumie* characterizes the force of a spiritual experience, very often an experience of the author himself.

These authors frequently surround the basic reinterpreted word with a series of synonyms, and of words close in meaning, creating in this way a "semantic field". Around the word "sleep" (*son*) are grouped the words "lulling to sleep" (*usyplenie*), "dream-vision" (*snovidenie*), "dream" (*mečta*), "dreaming" (*mečtanie*), even "delirium" (*bred*), etc. Contiguous to *mjatežnyj* are the words "stormy" (*burnyj*), "turbulent" (*bujnyj*), "agitation" (*volnenie*), in Glinka even "wavy" (*volnistyj*), "infuriated" (*razъjarennyj*), "implacable" (*neukrotimyj*), "savage" (*dikij*), etc. The antithetically-reinterpreted word pair "heat-cold" (*žar-cholod*), meaning sincerity and depth of spiritual experience, was already introduced into Russian poetry

[13] On this word see my review of H. W. Müller's dissertation *Das Musikalische in der Dichtung Lermontovs* in *ZfslPh.*, XIV (1936), 1-2, pp. 228–233.
[14] See my commentary to *Evgenij Onegin*, p. xxii.
[15] *Ibidem.*

by Sumarokov. The romanticists, and Puškin in particular, took up these words. Around the word *žar* is formed a semantic field of such words as "warm" (*teplo*), "fire" (*ogon'*), "flame" (*plamja*), "ardent" (*pylkij*), "boiling" (*kipjaščij*), etc.

It is interesting to note that the romantic poets, and especially Puškin, often group elements of one or several typical semantic fields into a single poem or into a single stanza or part of a long poem. There are many such places in *Evgenij Onegin* (stanzas III, 7, 24, 40; IV, 11; V, 30–31; VI, 36; VII, 2 and 23, etc.). About Lenskij's death, for example (VI, 36), we read:

> . . . Где жаркое волненье,
> где благородное стремленье
> и чувств и мыслей молодых,
> высоких, нежных, удалых?
> Где бурные любви желанья,
> и жажда знанья и труда,
> и страх порока и стыда,
> и вы, заветные мечтанья,
> вы, призрак жизни неземной,
> вы, сны поэзии святой!

"Where is the hot agitation, where the noble aspiration of youthful thoughts and feelings, lofty, tender, daring? Where are love's stormy longings, the thirst for toil and knowledge, the fear of vice and shame, and you, the sacred dreamings, you, the spectre of unearthly life, you, the dreams of holy poetry?"

(I space characteristic words of the semantic groups *son, mjatežnyj,* and *žar.*) We find just such places in Tjutčev and Vjazemskij (*cf.* the quotation above from the poem *Salovka*; this whole poem is full of romantic lexical elements). A similar role is played by the words gathered together in the poem "*To the Sea*" (*K Morju*) by Puškin:

> Прощай, свободная стихия!
> в последний раз передо мной
> ты катишь волны голубые
> и блещешь гордою красой.
> Как друга ропот заунывный,

как зов его в прощальный час,
твой грустный шум, твой шум призывный
услышал я в последний раз.

. . . .

Как я любил твои отзывы,
глухие звуки, бездны глас,
и тишину в вечерний час
и своенравные порывы.

"Farewell, free element! For the last time you roll before me your blue waves and sparkle in your proud beauty. Like the plaintive murmur of a friend, like his call at the hour of parting, I have heard for the last time your mournful sound, your invocation... How I loved your echoes, the muted sounds, the chasm's call and the silence at the evening hour, and the willful impulses."

Similar to this word complex of semantic fields connected with *svoboda*, *grust'*, and *bezdna*, is the mention of Byron:

исчез, оплаканный свободой...
... он духом создан был твоим:
как ты могущ, глубок и мрачен,
как ты, ничем неукротим...

"disappeared, by freedom mourned... he was created by thy spirit; as thou, puissant, deep, and somber, as thou indomitable."

In the same poem we meet such further expressions as "hidden intention" (*zavetnyj umysl*), "courageous" (*otvažno*), "indomitable" (*neodolimyj*), "the soul burst" (*rvalas' duša*), "storm's noise" (*buri šum*), "foul weather" (*nepogoda*), "murmur of the waves" (*govor voln*), and, antithetic to the above, "submissive" (*smirennyj*), "immovable" (*nepodvižnyj*), "fettered" (*okovan*), "tyrant" (*tiran*), "silent deserts" (*pustyni molčalivy*). Occasionally one and the same word is repeated (in *Evgenij Onegin* "trembling" [*trepetnyj*]).

The destiny of reinterpreted words is diverse. They often appear in a traditional context: thus, in Puškin's early poems, the words "sounds", "to sound", "noisy" (*zvuki, zvučat, zvučnyj*) are connected with the classical "lyre" (the poem *Kn. M. A. Golicynoj* mentioned above, 1823; *Jazykovu*, 1824). Furthermore, the word "lyre" follows the word *zvuki* and appears as a "commentary" to it.

40

Then the reinterpreted word begins to live its own life, appearing without commentary and in any context. The word *son* and its equivalents first appear with a direct explanation:

> сны поэзии святой...
> поэзии священный бред...

"The dreams of holy poetry,... poetry's sacred delirium..."

And then simply in a neutral vein, permitting the usual interpretation as well as the new:

> ... сладостный, безгрешный сон...
> ... сны задумчивой души...
> в каком он странном сне?

"...sweet, sinless sleep... dreams of the pensive soul... in what strange sleep is he?"

and so forth.

Reinterpreted words come to various ends. The semantic field of the word *son* remains "Puškinist" and finds almost no imitators, except for Vjazemskij, in whose work it is not infrequent, in Puškin's meaning, between 1829–49 (IV, pp. 57, 76, 115, 123, 187, 228, 350).[16] Vjazemskij also repeats the word *obman* in Puškin's sense (IV, 129, and again in 1854 in *P. F. Perfil'evoj*: "*obmanom tvorčeskoj duši*"). Some reinterpretations meet with more success. The field of the word *zvuki* completely drives out the "lyre" and ideas connected with it, in particular "I sing" (*poju*); however, beginning with the 'fifties of the nineteenth century, it is itself driven out by designations of poetry as "thoughts", "conceptions" (*dum, myslej*), etc., whereas the poet's activity is described by the word "I write" (*pišu*), found not only in Puškin but even in the eighteenth century. The word *bezumnyj* in its new coloration is not only maintained in poetry up to the epoch of symbolism (Bal'mont's "It's fine to be mad" [*prekrasno byt' bezumnym*]), but even penetrates the vocabulary of the broad masses, principally the half-educated. In Dostoevskij's *Selo Stepančikovo* a flirtatious

---

[16] Vjazemskij already uses the word "*obman*" in the new sense in the introduction to the first edition of Puškin's *Bachčisarajskij Fontan* (see *Sočinenija*, vol. I, 1878, p. 167–173).

girl taps a man on the shoulder with her fan and utters the word "madman" (*bezumec*), which in her opinion, of course, is not an insult, but a coquettish erotic challenge, a flirtation.

Only a broad historic investigation of the reinterpretation of words will provide a complete picture of their historic fate.[17]

There were other means of lexical extension in romantic poetry as well, of which the most important was the broadening of vocabulary by words borrowed from dialects, jargons (argot), and foreign languages. Such borrowings are often connected with particular circles of the people, with the imitation of folklore, and with the exoticism typical of romanticism. Slavic critics and literary historians have noticed these borrowings and often derived the tradition of romantic borrowings from Walter Scott. There may also be some influence of Victor Hugo. However, the majority of borrowings is explained by the necessity or rendering popular or exotic couleur locale. Such are the Ukrainian borrowings of Gogol' and the Polish "Ukrainian School" or of Słovacki. Eastern borrowings are legion in the Southern Poems of Puškin, in Mickiewicz's *Crimean Sonnets*, in Lermontov's Caucasian poems, in the literary prose of the orientalist Sen'kovskij, etc. We find dialectal elements in every romanticist who imitates or is interested in folklore. The large number of dialectisms in Mickiewicz's *Pan Tadeusz* is due to the local color he wished to lend his poem. A great many words now felt as dialectisms or rarities in the Jugoslav (Prešern, Preradović), Slovak (the whole school of Štur), and partly the Czech romanticists, are connected with the fact that these literary languages were then being created or renewed, and the

---

[17] There is a complex of words typical of romantic semantic fields in Vjazemskij's poem *K mnimoj sčastlivice* (1826); in the 30's and 40's we still find complexes of romantic words in the poems of poets of Stankevič's circle (Stankevič himself, I. Kljušnikov, V. Krasov). Corresponding word complexes are found in Macha's "nocturnal poems", in the Slovak poets of Štúr's school, and in the Polish romanticists. The words *plamja, plamennyj, vosplamenit'*, etc., applied to the emotions are already found in A. Sumarokov, A. Rževskij, and Batjuškov. It is highly probable that they are connected with French usage. Therefor this semantic field, typical of romanticism, is not new in Russian literature. It is essential, however, that words of this field have a different coloration in romanticism.

choice of lexical elements turned out to be different at a later time. It is an essential fact that this enrichment of the language by means of borrowings was connected with the romantic Weltanschauung, and in particular with the romantic conception of the poet as a free creator, not merely creating within one language, but having the right and even the obligation to form and renew the language itself. [18]

This is clearest of all in the creation of neologisms. These neologisms are not among those connected with the necessities of material or spiritual culture. The terminology of steamships and railroads was not created by poets. Nor was it poets who created words to signify new juridical conceptions nor even philosophic terminology: enthusiasm for the philosophy of Schelling may well have been a feature of the romantic epoch, but the poets, under the influence of this philosophy, created no new Slavic terminology. The neologisms of the Slavic romanticists belong to the sphere of poetic language and serve goals not of communication, but of art.

Since the neologisms of Slavic romanticists have not been sufficiently studied, I shall here dwell briefly upon those of the Russian romanticists.

The history of literary neologisms is notable for two particularities: in the first place, neologisms in large quantity are typical of certain literary epochs only, among which are the late baroque and the romantic. Secondly, neologisms are created almost exclusively by certain particular poets and writers, sometimes in the front ranks of literary life (Goethe, for example), sometimes little-noted and uninfluential, not only among wide circles of readers, but even in narrow literary circles, interested in every literary innovation (remarkable among the forgotten Slavic romanticists is the Slovak poet Samo Bohdan Hroboň).

Among the Russian romanticists, literary historians have noticed a large number of neologisms in the poems of V. Benediktov. Benediktov enjoyed a loud but brief success (approximately from 1835–45). His popularity diminished rapidly, although he remained a poet appreciated in narrow poets' circles and was not

[18] Eva Fiesel, *Die Sprachphilosophie der deutschen Romantik* (Tübingen, 1927), pp. 11 f., 137 ff., 190 ff.

completely forgotten by his readers. His collected poetry appeared after his death, in 1884 and 1902. The poet Ja. Polonskij, editor of these editions and biographer of Benediktov, added to his edition an "alphabetic list of words created by V. G. Benediktov, changed in form, or used by almost nobody, found in his works": [19] this list contains 143 words. Because of the lack of special studies of the neologisms of Benediktov's contemporaries and predecessors, of course, one cannot consider this list either complete or completely reliable. It is very difficult to establish the first appearance of one or the other word in a literary language, and particularly in the Russian literary language, since historians of Russian literature and the Russian literary language usually limit themselves to scrutinizing the vocabulary of certain of the more significant writers.

However, there are two creators of neologisms even among the better-known Russian romanticists. These are Boratynskij and Jazykov. The quantity of "rare words and neologisms" [20] in the first of these two writers reaches several dozen (about 80), in the second more than two hundred. We find an insignificant number of neologisms in Tjutčev. [21]

Among the neologisms of poetic language we can distinguish on the one hand those which an author uses constantly, apparently showing a desire to endow poetic speech with a new word, and on the other hand words which are created "*ad hoc*", out of the need to express a thought or emotion in a particular place in a literary work. In addition, one should distinguish between "strong" neologisms, that is those which it is difficult or impossible to understand without the corresponding explanation (in a literary work such an explanation is usually given by the context), and "weak"

[19]   So Ja. Polonskij calls his dictionary of Benediktov's neologisms (see the *Stichotvorenija* of Benediktov, SPb., 1902, vol. II, *Priloženie*, pp. i–iii).

[20]   There is a list of Boratynskij's neologisms and rare words in my materials, *Bibliografia i teksty k seminaru o kosvennych istočnikach istorii literatury* (Cambridge, Mass., 1952), p. 17; Jazykov's neologisms *ibidem*, pp. 18–20.

[21]   There are a few remarks on Tjutčev's neologisms in P. Brandt, 'Materialy k issledovaniju o poezii F. I. Tjutčeva', *IOPJa*, 1911, and separately. I take examples from the *Stichotvorenija* of Tjutčev in the edition *Bol'šaja Biblioteka Poèta*.

neolologisms, that is those which are intelligible to every reader, but unused, or not encountered in other poets and writers.

The neologisms of Benediktov and Boratynskij are almost all *"ad hoc"* creations, while in the poetry of Jazykov we find neologisms (a small number, it is true) which recur two or even three times. In my list of Jazykov's neologisms and rare words there are thirteen which recur (of which two are used three times) and which obviously belong to Jazykov's usual poetic vocabulary; they occur in poetry of various creative periods, very different from each other in character.

The weakest neologisms are double words. Such are Tjutčev's neologisms: *boleznenno-jarkij, volšebno-nemoj, bezljudno-veličavyj, proročeski-proščal'nyj, grustno-sirotejuščij,* etc. They are also found in Benediktov: *igrivo-gibkij, svetlo-zerkal'nyj, belo-krajnyj,*[22] etc. There are few in Boratynskij (*sedo-bradatyj, sladostno-tumannyj*), but a great many in Jazykov: *svobodno-odinokij, svobodno-šumnyj, nemiloserdno-samovlastnyj, prochladno-strastnyj, p'jano-bujnyj,* etc. Among them must be noticed a series of paradoxical neologisms, frequently appearing as oxymora: *pusto-veličavij, neprochodimo-besspokojnyj,* etc. Such is the character of Tjutčev's neologism, closely connected to the basic idea of the poem *"Insomnia"* (*Bessonica*), *proročeski-proščal'nyj.*

The "weakness" or "strength" of neologisms can be appraised basically subjectively. Another criterion, of course, can be the frequency in the language of other words, related by principles of word formation, their quantity and especially the productivity or non-productivity of the word-building elements in the structure of the neologism.

The following words can serve as examples of weak neologisms in Benediktov: *bezverec, bezmogil'nyj, neumjagčaemost', mrako-ljubec,* etc. Boratynskij has many words with the prefixes *bez-* and *ne-*, such as *neobščij, bezvesel'e,* and together with these *navestitel', gnetučij,* etc. There are also many weak neologisms in Jazykov: *nevoskovoj, nepoščadnyj, zabral'nyj, bezdiplomnyj, beskramol'nyj, brannoljubivyj, mnogovetvistyj, mnogogromnyj, mjatežničat', dušec-veten'e,* etc.

[22] Not "krajnij"!

45

Today, after the neologisms of Chlebnikov, Igor's Severjanin, and Majakovskij, we are no longer astounded by the strong neologisms of the romanticists. Benediktov has quite a number of them: *vskrepit'*, *golovosek* (sword), *zapancyrit'sja*, *zakrajna*, *zaezd* (ship), *zemnometatel'*, *zaljubovnyj*, *kainstvo*, *netoptatel'*, *otčuždenec*, *perelomka*, *prostoroždenec*, *predvkusie* (usually *predvkušenie*), *razviv*, *sogreva*, *utiš'e*, *čelovečit'sja*, etc. There are fewer in Boratynskij: *perechodnaja* (*p. zvezda*, "planet"), *bratstvovat'*, *obniknut'*; very many in Jazykov: *raznobojarščina*, *kričal'ščik*, *stolbnica*, *pomoga*, *peretoskovat'*, *podaren'ice*, *lošadinnik*, *obnemečit'*, *pereočkat'*, *čužemyslitel'*, *mjasničat'*, etc. I shall not explain these strong neologisms here: in the majority of cases, wothout knowing the context, the reader would either not unpuzzle their meaning or interpret them incorrectly.

Jazykov's neologisms attracted the attention of his contemporaries: in 1844 N. A. Nekrasov published two parodies, among the most successful of Russian literature;[23] in them we meet both neologisms of Jazykov himself and a good many others formed according to Jazykov's models.

Aside from neologisms in the regular sense of the term, we find in Jazykov no small number of cases where ordinary words are used in a not entirely ordinary or completely extra-ordinary sense: his *pustynnaja sinica* means a titmouse found in the desert; a *dorožnyj poet* means a wandering poet, etc.[24]

In any case the neologisms of the romanticists are one of their methods of linguistic creation, and their linguistic creation is not accidental, but is bound to their conception of the tasks and rights of the poet.

Unusual word combinations, examples of which we have just seen in Jazykov, and another example of which might be Vjazemskij's unusual metaphor comparing the waterfall's waves with volcanic lava (*cf.* above), are also one of the means of renovating the

[23] Nekrasov, *Poslanie k sosedu* and *Poslanie k drugu iz-za granicy* (1844 and 1845), *Sobranie Sočinenij*, vol. I (1949), pp. 377ff. The second *poslanie* is reprinted in abridged form in my Materials (*cf.* note 21), pp. 37–8.

[24] There are similar constructions in the poems of Mácha: see the beginning of the poem *Máj*, "večerní máj" instead of "majovy večer".

language. These word combinations often recall the baroque *concetti*. Oxymora, formed by rapprochement of water with fire or of heat with cold or fire with frost, are not infrequent in baroque poetry (in the Slavic, for example, in A. Morsztyn).[25] Study of original romantic word combinations in general has yet to be begun.

[25] *Cf.* my commentary to *Evgenij Onegin*, p. 257 (snow and heat); there is an identification of "snow" and "coal" (*sneg, pepel*) in Vjazemskij (So*č*inenija, vol. IV, 1880, p. 291).

ANTIRATIONALISM — MADNESS —
"PREJUDICES"

To the most essential traits of the romantic world-view belong opposition both to classical poetics and to the rationalism of the eighteenth-century Enlightenment. Connected with just this second trait are both the fantastic in romantic poetry (especially ballads) and a series of word reinterpretations, in particular, among those already mentioned, the reinterpretation of the words "heart" and "madness" (*serdce, bezumie*).

The word *serdce*, of course, is a constant unit of the poetic lexicon; its usual use as a simple contrast to the "head" is an opposition between the emotions and the intelligence. In this meaning the word *serdce* becomes a particularly frequent lexical element in Russian "sentimentalism", the school of Karamzin, which is stylistically only a modification of classicism. The works of Karamzin, I. T. Dmitriev, and the young Žukovskij are full of this word. It is not infrequent even in the works of the older classicists. However, this word too is reinterpreted in romanticism. The reinterpretation of the word *serdce* tends to broaden its functions: the "heart" is the bearer not only of the emotions, but also of cognitive faculties, and furthermore of a cognition more profound than that of the pure intelligence. On the other hand, the "heart" is the source of creativity, the source of images of the fantasy, but also of thoughts. Finally, the "heart" is a symbol of that profound realm of the human spirit, of that "abyss" which is hidden beneath the surface of commonplace, everyday experience. In this latter mert"aning the word "hea is close to the conception of the "inner man" (*vnutrennij čelovek*) of the Church Fathers and of mysticism of all times.[1] The word "heart" in the romanticists' reinterpretation adjoins the semantic fields of "sleep" (*son*) on the one hand and "abyss" (*bezdna*) on the other. It is precisely this adjunction which explains the origin of the word combination "depth of the hearts" (*serdečnaja glubina*), which we discussed above.[2]

It is characteristic that one of the principal program works of Slavic romanticism is Mickiewicz's *Romantyczność*, a poem which is both a proclamation that the heart is the source of cognition and an apology of madness. The poem's content is not complicated. A girl speaks with her deceased sweetheart, whom she sees before here as if alive. When the shade of her beloved disappears with the dawn, a crowd is attracted by the girl's cry: "Pray!" resound the voices, "that was his soul." Only one old man – a representative of the Enlightenment – declares the girl's vision to be delirium and belief in spirits to be the fruit of stupidity and a blasphemy against reason. The author remains at the edge of the crowd:

"Dziewczyna czuje, – odpowiadam skromnie –
a gawiedź wierzy głęboko;
czucie i wiara silniej mówi do mnie
niż mędrca szkiełko i oko.

Martwe znasz prawdy, nieznane dla ludu,
widzisz świat w proszku, w każdej gwiazd iskierce:
nie znasz prawd żywych, nie obazysz cudu!
Miej serce i patrzaj w serce!"

[1] *Cf.* chapter 3, note 29.

[2] *Cf.* chapter 3 above, on Žukovskij. "*V glubine serdca*" is still found in the usual sense in Puškin's drafts of *Bachčisarajskij Fontan*. The meaning of the expressions "*iz glubiny duši*" and "*vo glubinu duši*" is unclear in N. Gnedič's poem *K drugu* 2 (1819, *Sočinenija*, SPb., 1905, I, p. 82). Kozlov's words "*tajna serdca*" (*Drugu Žukovskomu*, 1822) and "*v pylu serdečnych upoenij*" (*K Italii*, 1828) are explained by the context. Cf. also in A. A. Šiškov (1799–1832), *31 dekabrja 1828 g.* (*Moskovskij Vestnik*, 1830, 2, 7; not in the *Sočinenija* of Šiškov, 1834–5): "*v serdečnoj glubine zažžeš' li svetoč radosti i mira*". The expression of Batjuškov "*pamjat' serdca*" (*Mysli*, *Vestnik Evropy*, 1810, 13; *Sočinenija*, ed. L. Majkov, II, 35; *O lučšich svojstvach serdca*, 1815, *Sočinenija*, II, pp. 142ff.; the poem *Moj Genij*, 1816), as is clear from the author's own explanations, is borrowed from French literature and in meaning does not depass the boundaries of sentimentalism. Later readers have been introducing a romantic meaning into the lines of the poem *Moj Genij*.

"I answer humbly: a maiden feels, but the crowd believes profoundly; feeling and faith speak more strongly to me than the eye and the glass of the sage. You know dead truths, unknown to the people, you see the world in a speck of dust, in every sparklet of the stars: you know not living truths, you will not see the marvel! Have a heart and look into the heart!"

Thus Mickiewicz's *Romantyczność* ends with a proclamation of doubt about the Enlightenment's view of reality, recognition of the justice of the crowd's "prejudices", and affirmation of the rights of the "heart" as a cognitive organ. At the moment when this poem appeared in a collection of Mickiewicz's ballads (1822), these ideas had already been widely disseminated by West European romanticism. Mickiewicz's ballad must have impressed any reader not partisan to the romantic world-view as an apology of madness, and was in fact considered as such.

Mickiewicz's ballad was echoed in other Slavic literatures, and not only in the period of early romanticism, the twenties and thirties. As late as the forties, the most romantic of the Slovak poets, Janko Kráľ, repeats in one of his early poems the ideas of Mickiewicz's *Romantyczność*:

> Nečulým srdciam svet je zatvorený,
> ten, kto necíti, ten je vylúčený
> zo sveta, a len pri bráne sa tára,
> ktorému sa ta nikdy neotvára.
> Je dačo tajno na tom šírom svete,
> o čom vy, zemskí mudrci, neviete –
> čoho, keď druhým v oči sa podíva,
> zlaknú sa vraviac: to sa nám len sníva.

"The world is closed to hearts which do not feel, he who feels not is excluded from the world and only knocks on doors which to him will never open. There is a secret something in this wide world which you, o wordly sages, do not know – of which you, looking another in the eyes, are terrified, saying, we only dream this."

In 1861 an epigon of Ukrainian romanticism, P. Kuliš, published a translation of *Romantyczność* ending with the words:

> Ти у небо прозираєш
> і в землю глибоко,

> а без серця в чуже серце
> не заглянеш оком!

"You see deep into the sky and earth, but without a heart you cannot see into another's heart."

and the following year printed a collection of original poems, *Dosvitky*, in which he plays endless variations on the theme of the heart as a bearer not only of the emotions, but also of cognition, tradition, nationality, etc. Kuliš' world-view, developed in poetic works during the next ten years, is concentrated about the heart symbol more consistently than that of any other Slavic romantic poet.[3] In this same way the German romanticist and romantic psychologist Justinus Kerner, at the end of his literary career, translates *Romantycznosc*, which he considers one of the most characteristic works of romanticism.[4]

However, the word *serdce*, as already mentioned, began its journey even before the ballad of Mickiewicz. More noteworthy than the fate of the word *serdce* is that of several conceptions, the evaluation of which changed completely in romanticism. These conceptions, related to that same antirationalism which was always connected with the heart symbol, are those of "madness" and "prejudice" (*bezumie, predrassudok*).

Madmen played almost no role in classicist literature. One can find several images of madmen, primarily in adventure novels, where they appear as laughable, comic figures. A completely different role is assigned to them in romantic literature. Madness uncovers the essential in the human soul, removes the cover from the secret motives which are hidden in everyday life. Such is the fate of German in Puškin's *Pikovaja Dama* and of Popriščin in Gogol's *Zapiski Sumasšedšego*. However, madness also uncovers to man certain depths of cognition inaccessible to him in a normal

---

[3] On the "philisophy of the heart" of P. Kuliš see my article 'P. O. Kuliš, ein ukrainischer Philosoph des Herzens', *Orient und Occident*, XIV (1933), pp. 1–18, and *Narysy* . . . (see chapter 3, note 29), pp. 119–128.
[4] The translation of *Romantyczność* is in Justinus Kerner, *Der letzte Blumenstrauss* (1852), under the title "Erscheinung"; Kerner's letters about *Romantyczność* are in F. Pocci jun., *Justinus Kerner und sein Münchner Freudenkreis* (Berlin, 1928), pp. 245 and 247.

state. Evgenij in Puškin's *Mednyj Vsadnik* rises, in just such a state of madness, to the point where he becomes a spokesman of the problem of the philosophy of history which interests Puškin in this poem: the contradiction between individual happiness and the great events of the historic process. In *Poltava* Maria's eyes are opened, in a state of insanity, to the character of Mazepa (as the poet wished to depict him). Nor must one forget the mad scene of Dubrovskij's father in court: in the language of insanity he characterizes his judges better than this could have been done in the language of a normal accusation. The *jurodivyj* in *Boris Godunov* is the only character in the play who speaks frankly of the crime of Car' Boris. Also worthy of attention is the madness of Mel'nik in *Rusalka*. [5]

We can even find a direct apology of madness in Puškin, in the poem "*God keep me from going mad*" (*Ne daj mne Bog sojti s uma* 1833). The poem's content is diametrically opposed to this first line; he declares openly:

> Не то, что б разумом моим
> я дорожил; не то чтоб с ним
> расстаться был не рад...

"Not that I prize my reason, not that I should not be glad to part with it."

In the poet's opinion, insanity would bring him to a peculiar intimacy and merging with nature:

> Когда б оставили меня
> на воле, как бы резво я
> пустился в темный лес!

> Я пел бы в пламенном бреду,
> я забывался бы в чаду,
> нестройных, чудных грез.

> И я б заслушивался волн,
> и я глядел бы, счастья полн,
> в пустые небеса.

[5] See the articles cited in chapter 3, note 28.

И силен, волен был бы я,
как вихорь роющий поля,
ломающий леса...

"had I been left in freedom, how quickly had I fled into the dark forest! I should have sung in fiery delirium, lost myself in the daze of disordered, wondrous fancies. I should delight in hearing the waves and, replete with joy, stare into the empty heavens. And I should be strong and free, as the whirlwind, rooting up fields and smashing forests..."

The line "*Ne daj mne Bog sojti s uma*" is motivated in the poem only by the attitude of society towards the madman:

как раз тебя запрут,
посадят на цепь дурака,
и сквозь решетку, как зверка,
дразнить тебя прдиут...

"But they'll just lock you up, put you on a chain, a fool, and they'll come to tease you through the grille, an animal."

However, Russian literature also contains a direct apology of madness, in the remarkable collection of romantic tales of prince V. Odoevskij *The Russian nights* (*Rosskie Noči* written in the thirties, published in 1840). This collection of stories, according to Odoevskij's original plan, should have borne the title *The madhouse* (*Dom Sumasšedšich*). [6] Odoevskij's friends and contemporaries were vitally interested in this plan of his (as early as 1833). [7] The theme of insanity was preserved during the writing and publication of the separate tales which were to enter *Dom Sumasšedšich*, but the title was changed to *Russkie Noči*; it is possible that Odoevskij did this because, during the years of preparation of the collection, other articles appeared which anticipated the title of his book: N. Polevoj's story *The felicity of folly* (*Blaženstvo bezumija* in *Moskovskij Telegraf*, 1833, Nos. 1 and 2) and article *The mad and the non-mad* (*Sumasšedšie i ne-sumasšedšie*, collection *Novyj Živopisec*..., vol. III, 1832). Polevoj with his notion of the "abyss of the soul"

[6] P. Sakulin, *op. cit.*, II, pp. 203 ff.
[7] Letter of Gogol' to I. I. Dmitriev, 30 November 1832 (Academy edition, vol. X, 1940, pp. 247–8) and of Pletnev to Žukovskij, 8 December 1832 (*Sočinenija* of Pletnev, vol. III, 1885, p. 522), further in Sakulin, II, p. 203, note 1.

(*bezdna duši*) was in general attracted by the theme of madness. [8]
In 1835 appears a translation of the article of I. Goerres *The mad-house, or, Ideas about art and mental disturbance* (*Dom sumasšedšich ili idei ob iskusstve i pomešatel'stve uma, Moskovskij nabljudatel'*, 1835, 4). This article, written after 1826, is a commentary to the painting "The Madhouse" of Wilhelm Kaulbach, with whom Goerres had become friendly in Munich. In this article Goerres outlines his romantic views of the essence of art and interprets Kaulbach's painting. In Goerres' opinion, forms of madness are symptoms of the illness of contemporary society, of the "fallen humanity" of this times. According to Goerres, Kaulbach portrayed madmen typical of his times. Both the insane and the indifferent superintendant in Kaulbach's painting are in Goerres' opinion typical representatives of contemporary European life; all the aspects of insanity portrayed in the painting are but reflections of contemporary interests (political adventurism, revolutionary enthusiasms, market speculation, prostitution, etc.). Odoevskij was undoubtedly impressed by the discussions of insanity in the Serapionsbrüder of E. Th. A. Hoffmann: here, as in the article of Polevoj (*cf.* above), who was perhaps writing under the influence of *Serapionsbrüder*, the question is put as to just where the boundary lies between insanity and normality. In 1836 Odoevskij himself publishes an article *Who is the madman?* (*Kto sumasšedšij? Biblioteka dlja čtenija*, 1836, vol. 14): this is a first edition of the introduction to *Dom Sumasšedšich*. Here Odoevskij remarks only that the "crowd" is ready to consider people insane who are distinguished by an inquisitive spirit and who doubt the generally accepted "truths". The heroes of this story-article are placed in the eighteenth century, undoubtedly because the "truths" of the Age of Enlightenment seemed to Odoevskij to be mistakes and delusions. Thus the supposedly "insane" critics of the ideas of the Enlightenment are in reality normal, and their opponents should be considered insane. ...

In a reworked form this article became a part of *Russkie Noči*. *Russkie Noči* is a collection of tales, framed by the conversation of several friends. Odoevskij places his own ideas in the mouth of one

---

[8] V. Orlov, *N. A. Polevoj* (1934), pp. 300–301 (memoirs of K. Polevoj).

of the friends, to whom he gives the name of "Russian Faust". In his mouth are placed the second night (*Noč' vtoraja*) and the repetition of the story-article *Kto sumasšedšij?*. Odoevskij, the Russian Faust, beginning with an ironical exposition of the attainments of the Age of Enlightenment, goes over to questions of principle. First of all he observes that science, having attained the "highest degree of perfection", is becoming incomprehensible to both the simple and the noble man. The highest thoughts of the sages turn out to be incomprehensible to the "lower" classes, who "accuse the upper of insanity". And this accusation is not completely unjust. First of all "it is impossible to draw a true, fixed line between healthy and insane thought". A series of examples proves that scientific theories are often by their nature hardly distinguished from the ideas of the insane. Not only that, but the condition of the madman is similar to the spiritual condition of the poet and of any genial inventor. In both madman and genius all completely disparate ideas are concentrated about one point. Both madman and genius must "sacrifice thousands of notions, generally accepted and apparently correct", and therefore every new idea – of the madman or of the genius – seems at the first moment to be "delirium". "There is no great man who, at the moment of conception in him of a new discovery, would not seem insane." Such is the similarity between insanity and genius from the point of view of the entourage. But the "exalted" state of the genius, itself, is closer to what is called madness than madness is to "ordinary animal stupidity". "That which we call madness, an ecstatic state, delirium, is this not at times the highest degree of human mental instinct, a degree so high that it becomes completely incomprehensible, imperceptible to ordinary observation?" This is not contradicted even by the notion that mental illness is a disease of the brain: it is possible that the brain, in just such a diseased state, is capable of fulfilling those tasks which it could not fulfill in a normal condition. . . .

Such, fundamentally, are the conceptions of Odoevskij. The very idea of the lack of a border between insanity and normality, of the lack of criteria for distinguishing between them, is utilized later by Herzen in his *Doktor Krupov* (1847), of course in a completely different interpretation and with a satiric goal,[9] and we still meet echoes of this idea in Čechov's tale *Palata nomer šestoj*.

On the following pages of *Russkie Noči* Odoevskij placed, among others, several tales illustrating by examples the proximity of genius to insanity. These are the tales devoted to Giambatista Piranesi (*Noč' tret'ja*), Beethoven (*Poslednij kvartet Betchovena, Noč' šestaja*), and Bach (*Sebastijan Bach, Noč' vos'maja*). These three tales are organically woven into the composition of *Russkie Noči*, which is devoted to the development of the romantic Weltanschauung and particularly to the critique of contemporary society and of positivist science.[10]

In a certain sense the genial heroes of *Russkie Noči* are abnormal, "insane", since in each of them genius has distorted the normal structure of the human psyche. To Piranesi, Bach, and Beethoven must be joined the imaginary hero of a further tale of *Russkie Noči*, *Improvizator*. Odoevskij goes further in the story *Kosmorama*, which originated after the four above-mentioned stories of *Russkie Noči*:[11] the hero of *Kosmorama* seems to others and even to himself "insane", not because of some defect, but on the contrary because of his particular "astral wisdom" (*zvëzdnaja mudrost'*), his ability to penetrate more deeply into reality than could a normal man.

---

[9] It is possible that the *Russkie Noči* had some influence on the origin of Herzen's story; the latter was by his own admission "strongly influenced" by "Bach", for example (Sakulin, *Odoevskij*, I, 2, p. 430).

[10] *Russkie Noči* appeared in 1840. In that same year the theme of insanity is touched upon in the story *Meščanin* of A. Bašuckij (SPb., 1840) and in the following year in *Ispoved'* of I. M. Jastrebcev (SPb., 1841; noted by Sakulin, II, p. 205, note 1). As was already mentioned E. Th. A. Hoffman undoubtedly influenced *Russkie Noči*. It is especially worth mentioning the tale *Ritter Glück*, in which the famous composer is drawn in traits similar to Odoevskij's Beethoven and Bach. It is interesting to note that Gogol' intended to write a *Zapiski sumasšedšego muzykanta* (*Sočinenija* of Gogol', ed. Tichonravov, vol V, pp. 610–611); this plan was abandoned in favor of the *Zapiski sumasšedšego* in *Arabeski* (1834). Gogol' was in general interested in abnormal manifestations of spiritual life, as is affirmed by the letter of I. A. Fonvizin (1849) printed in *Literaturnoe Nasledstvo*, 58 (1953), p. 715; unfortunately, Gogol's story of a girl suffering from hallucinations is omitted.

[11] *Kosmorama* was printed in *Otečestvennye Zapiski*, 1840, 8. The stories mentioned above first appeared: *Poslednij kvartet Betxovena* in 1831 (*Severnye cvety*), *Piranezi* in 1832 (*Severnye cvety*), *Improvizator* in 1833 (the almanach *Al'ciona*), *Bach* in 1835 (*Moskovskij Nabljudatel'*, 1835, 5).

The apology of madness is connected in Odoevskij's work with other motifs, and in particular with the antirationalist thesis of the positive content of that which the eighteenth-century Enlightenment considered "prejudices" and "superstitions" (*predrassudki, sueverija*). As is well known, the Enlightenment considered everything as "prejudices" to which it was impossible, as it seemed, to attribute a rational basis: here was relegated everything resting upon tradition.... Particularly characteristic is the relation of the Enlightenment to the "conventions" of religious rites. And from these "senseless conventions" there was an easy transition to the bases of religion in general. Writers of the Enlightenment (for example Voltaire) fought against "prejudices" by the method of "*ostranenie*".[12] It seemed to them that destroying prejudices would open the way to the creation of a positive and intelligent spiritual culture. As is well known, the enlighteners themselves, in the course of this critique, not infrequently fell victim of illusion ("optical illusion"[13]). Such was Voltaire's denial of the finding of fossilized sea life, since he saw in these finds proof that there had been a universal Flood; such are Lichtenberg's gibes at the theory of the cosmic origin of meteorites and his doubting even the fact that meteorites fall: these facts reminded him too much of Biblical stories of "rains of stone". And so forth.

Odoevskij defends even legends of magic and charms. "Legends have been preserved: when man was really the king of nature; when each creature obeyed his voice, because he could name it; when all the forces of nature, as humble slaves, crawled at the feet of men" (*Russkie Noči: Noč' vtoraja*[14]). Odoevskij was convinced that primitive man possessed an instinct ("instinctive force") which gave him a knowledge deeper than our rational knowledge.

[12] About "*ostranenie*" see my remarks in 'Comenius' Labyrinth of theWorld: its themes and their sources', *Harvard Slavic Studies*, I (1953), pp. 117–127. *Ibidem* are several indications of literature on this question. The concept itself, as it seems, was already outlined in Aristotle's *Poetics* (Chapter 22, 1458a, 20ff., about the meaning of strange – ξενικός – expressions; *cf. ibidem* on the meaning of surprises in a poetic work, chapter 9, and a positive evaluation of confusion in the action of a tragedy, chapter 13).

[13] *Cf.* Chapter 2, note 15.

[14] *Russkie Noči* (Moscow, 1913), p. 64.

"Primitive man must have known Nature better than our modern man, just as the bees understand the advantages of the hexagon".[15] The strengthening of man's rational capacities leads to a diminution of the strength of instinct. Even now there exist "remains" of instinctive knowledge – "they were great, and in this sense the ancients knew more than modern man". The mission of humanity is the "synthesis" of instinct and reason.[16]

The romantic poets step forth in defense of prejudices with complete certainty. One can hardly mention Puškin's "superstitions" in this connection; we do not know with certainty his opinions of these superstitions.[17] Boratynskij, however, left two striking poems on this theme. One of them recalls closely the above-mentioned section of *The Russian nights* (*Russkie Noči*). This poem was written at the same time that *Russkie Noči* appeared in print (1840); it bears the title "*Signs*" (*Primety*):

> Пока человек естества не пытал
> горнилом, весами и мерой;
> но детски вещаньям природы внимал,
> ловил ее знаменья с верой;

> Покуда природу любил он, она
> любовью ему отвечала:
> О нем дружелюбной заботы полна,
> язык для него обретала.

"As long as man did not try nature with crucible, scale, and measure; childlike he heard the prophecies of nature, seized her signs with faith; as long as he loved nature, she responded to him in love: full of friendly care for him, she found a tongue for him (to understand)."

[15] Odoevskij, 'Psichologičeskie zametki', *Sovremennik*, XXXII (1843), and addenda from manuscripts, given by Sakulin in *Odoevskij*, I, 1, pp. 469–72.
[16] 'Pis'ma k grafine E.P.R(ostopčin)oj o prividenijach . . .' (Odoevskij, *Sočinenija*, vol. III, 1844, pp. 307–359; earlier in *Otečestvennya Zapiski*, 1839, 1 and 2. On these views of Odoevskij see V. Zen'kovskij, *Istorija russkoj filosofii*, I, Paris, 1948, pp. 149f., 151f.).
[17] One can also recall Puškin's *Primety* (1829). Material about Puškin's superstition is collected in S. Stein's uncritical *Puškin mistik* (Riga, 1931) (cf. my review in *Put'*, No. 32, 1932). Cf. the article of Bishop Ioann (Šachovskij) in *Novoe Russkoe Slovo*, 5 June 1955: 'Puškin i potustoronnee'.

This language consisted in "signs": the raven's croak predicted misfortune and forced man to abstain from his intention, the appearance of a wolf before troops leaving on campaign foretold victory, a pair of doves hovering above a man promised him the "bliss of love"...

> В пустыне безлюдной он не был одним,
> нечуждая жизнь в ней дышала.
>
> Но чувство презрев, он доверил уму;
> вдался в суету изысканий...
> И сердце природы закрылось ему,
> и нет на земле прорицаний.

"In the solitary wilderness he was not alone, there breathed in it a not-unfamiliar life. But disdaining feeling, he trusted intellect; entered into the vanity of research... And the heart of nature closed itself to him, and on earth there are no prophecies."

This poem corresponds even in detail to Odoevskij's manuscript *Psychological remarks* (*Psichologičeskie zametki*) about the "fabulous legends of old" and the "instinctive strength" of primitive man. Moreover, we read exactly the same thing in the lines of Seweryn Goszczyński:

> Ależ bo wówczas — ziemio staroświecka! —
> dzisiejsze dziwy dziwamy nie były;
> grały widomie niewidome sily
> i pilnowaly człowieka, jak dziecka.
> W powietrzu, w drzewach, w kamienu, pod wodą
> krewne spółczucie ludzie znajdowali,
> bo nie gardzili naówczas przyroda,
> bo ją, jak matkę, znali i kochali.

"But at one time – the earth is ancient – today's miracles were not miracles; invisible forces played visibly and cared for man as for a child. In the air, the trees, the stone, beneath the water, people found a kindred sympathy, for then they did not scorn nature, but knew and loved her as a mother."

(*Sobótka*, 1837). In the following year, after *Signs*, Boratynskij writes a poem frankly dedicated to "Prejudice". He, it is true, does not step forth as a defender of "prejudices", but he considers them relics of former truths, and his appeal for impartiality toward prejudices signifies only the need of understanding their meaning *in the past:*

> Предрассудок! он обломок
> давней правды. Храм упал;
> а руин его — потомок
> языка не разгадал.
>
> Гонит в нем наш век надменный,
> не узнав его лица,
> нашей правды современной
> дряхлолетнего отца...

"Prejudice! It is a fragment of ancient truth. The temple fell; the descendents have not unriddled the language of its ruins. In it our haughty century pursues, not having recognized his face, the ancient father of our modern truth."

And Boratynskij's poem ends with an appeal to respect prejudices:

> Воздержи младую силу!
> Дней его не возмущая;
> но пристойную могилу,
> как уснет он, предку дай.

"Hold back young force! trouble not his days; but, when he dies, give this ancestor a wortky grave."

Tjutčev repeats the same thought. In the early poem *A.N.M.* (1821), even before he joined the circle of Odoevskij (the "Ljubomudry", 1823), Tjutčev defends the antirationalist view of nature by purely aesthetic emotional arguments:

> Нет веры вымыслам чудесным,
> рассудок все опустошил
> и, покорив законам тесным
> и воздух, и моря, и сущу,
> как пленников их обнажил;
> ту жизнь до дна он иссушил,

что в дерево вливала душу,
давала тело бестелесным!...

. . . .

"There is no faith in wondrous legends, reason has devastated all and,
subjugating to narrow laws the air and sea and land, like captives has
disrobed them; it dried out that life, that instilled a soul into the tree
and gave a body to the immaterial!..."

Tjutčev, perhaps remembering Schiller's *Die Götter Griechenlands*,
believes that "ancient peoples" regarded nature differently:

Ваш мир был храмом всех богов,
вы книгу матери-природы
читали ясно, без очков...

"Your world was a temple of all gods, you read the book of mother
nature clearly, without glasses..."

The argument in favor of the world-view of the "ancient peoples",
who animated the world, is however purely aesthetic:

О раб ученой суеты
и скованный своей наукой!
Напрасно, критик, гонишь ты
их златокрылые мечты;
поверь — сам опыт в том порукой —
чертог волшебный добрых фей
и в сновиденьи веселей,
чем наяву томиться скукой
в убогой хижине твоей!...

"O slave of learned vanity, enchained by your own science! In vain,
o critic, you pursue their golden-winged dreams; Believe – experience
is guarantee of that – the magic palace of good fairies is even in dream
more merry than, awake, to languish in boredom in your squalid hut!...."

The "golden-winged dreams", as compared to the world-view of
rationalist science, have the advantage only of giving man a more
joyous existence, even though this existence be a "dream". Ten
years later Tjutčev, having passed through the "school" of Odoevskij's circle and having become acquainted with German roman-

ticism, speaks much more decidedly (in the poem *Ne to, čto mnite vy...*, post 1830):

> Не то, что мните вы, природа:
> не слепок, не бездушный лик, —
> в ней есть душа, в ней есть свобода,
> в ней есть любовь, в ней есть язык...

"Not what you think, is nature; no mould, no soulless image, – it has a soul, has freedom, has love, has a tongue..."

Echoes of Schelling's philosophy are clear in these lines. And for the opponents of such a view of nature Tjutčev finds much more decisive words:

> Они не видят и не слышат,
> живут в сем мире, как в потьмах...
>
> . . . .
>
> Лучи к ним в душу не сходили,
> весна в груди их не цвела,
> при них леса не говорили
> и ночь в звездах нема была.
>
> И языками неземными,
> волнуя реки и леса,
> в ночи не совещалась с ними
> в беседе дружеской гроза!
>
> Не их вина: пойми, коль может,
> органа жизнь, глухонемой!
> Души его, ах, не встревожит
> и голос матери самой!

"They do not see and do not hear, they live in this world as if in darkness... No rays came down into their souls, no Springtime bloomed within their breast, near them the forests did not speak, and the night in stars was still. And disturbing rivers and woods with supernal tongues, at night the storm did not confer with them in friendly discourse! Not theirs the guilt: let the deaf-mute understand as best he can the organ's life! His soul, alas, will not be roused by his very mother's voice!"

Tjutčev is echoed by a member of that same romantic group, D. Venevitinov: not quite clearly in the rough draft *Morning*, *midday, evening and night (Utro, polden', večer i noč')*, written in 1825.[18] He develops the same thoughts during that year in a letter to Košelev[19] in "primitive man all feelings were thoughts, therefore he knew all", "when philosophy was born, man lost touch with nature". Unexpectedly, we find these same ideas in Russian religious thinkers of the 20th century.[20]

These are but a few fragments of the poetic polemics of the romantic poets. By their vocabulary alone they lead one off to a series of further themes, which I shall not discuss here. The defense of prejudices, in whatever form it is carried on, leads the romantics' thought to romantic natural philosophy, to the philosophy of history with its notion of a "golden age" at the beginning of history,[21] to problems of folklore, and to the romantic theory of cognition.... However, the question of the sources of the Weltanschauung of the Slavic romantic poets means dealing with German romanticism, with mysticism of the middle ages and of modern times, and in particular with Russian masonic mysticism, and finally with the sources of middle-age and modern mysticism in the philosophy of the church fathers and in Platonism.

---

[18]   Venevitinov, *Polnoe Sobranie Sočinenij* (1934), pp. 130–31. A rough copy was first printed in the almanach *Uranija*, 1826.

[19]   *Idem.*, p. 301.

[20]   S. N. Bulgakov, *Svet nevečernij* (Moscow, 1917), p. 230 and remark 1 thereto, where the author speaks of the "natural ability of man to penetrate beneath the crust of appearances", and even more clearly on p. 326: "Paganism, thanks to its mystic vision, saw 'gods' there where to our scientific sense only 'natural forces' are accessible".

[21]   On the "Golden Age" see W. Lettenbauer, 'Das Bild der aetas aurea bei A. Delvig', *Festschrift für D. Cyževśkyj* (Berlin, 1954), pp. 164–170. The very concept of a "Golden Age" belonged in the middle ages to the literary *loci communes* (it is found in Russian literature in the 16th century in the *poslanie* of Fedor Karpov to the Metropolite Daniil); this conception is reinterpreted by romanticism and encountered frequently in the German romantics as a designation of the primary condition of humanity, but also of the impending age of flowering of poetry; it is also not infrequent in the Russian romanticists.